Business Ethics and Society Exam

About Peterson's

Peterson's has been your trusted educational publisher for more than 50 years. It's a milestone we're quite proud of, as we continue to offer the most accurate, dependable, high-quality educational content in the field, providing you with everything you need to succeed. No matter where you are on your academic or professional path, you can rely on Peterson's for its books, online information, expert test-prep tools, the most up-to-date education exploration data, and the highest quality career success resources—everything you need to achieve your education goals. For our complete line of products, visit **www.petersons.com.**

For more information, contact Peterson's, 4380 S. Syracuse St., Suite 200, Denver, CO 80237; 800-338-3282 Ext. 54229; or visit us online at **www.petersons.com.**

ISBN-13: 978-0-7689-4440-2

Printed in the United States of America

10 9 8 7 6 5 4 3 2 1   24 23 22

Contents

Before You Begin

HOW THIS BOOK IS ORGANIZED

Peterson's *Master the™ DSST® Business Ethics and Society Exam* provides a diagnostic test, subject-matter review, and a post-test.

- **Diagnostic Test**—Twenty multiple-choice questions, followed by an answer key with detailed answer explanations
- **Assessment Grid**—A chart designed to help you identify areas that you need to focus on based on your test results
- **Subject-Matter Review**—General overview of the exam subject, followed by a review of the relevant topics and terminology covered on the exam
- **Post-test**—Sixty multiple-choice questions, followed by an answer key and detailed answer explanations

The purpose of the diagnostic test is to help you figure out what you know—or don't know. The twenty multiple-choice questions are similar to the ones found on the DSST exam, and they should provide you with a good idea of what to expect. Once you take the diagnostic test, check your answers to see how you did. Included with each correct answer is a brief explanation regarding why a specific answer is correct, and in many cases, why other options are incorrect. Use the assessment grid to identify the questions you miss so that you can spend more time reviewing that information later. As with any exam, knowing your weak spots greatly improves your chances of success.

Following the diagnostic test is a subject-matter review. The review summarizes the various topics covered on the DSST exam. Key terms are defined; important concepts are explained; and when appropriate, examples are provided. As you read the review, some of the information may seem familiar while other information may seem foreign. Again, take note of the unfamiliar because that will most likely cause you problems on the actual exam.

After studying the subject-matter review, you should be ready for the post-test. The post-test contains sixty multiple-choice items, and it will serve as a dry run for the real DSST exam. There are complete answer explanations at the end of the test.

OTHER DSST® PRODUCTS BY PETERSON'S

Books, flashcards, practice tests, and videos available online at **www.petersons.com/testprep/dsst.**

- A History of the Vietnam War
- Art of the Western World
- Astronomy
- Business Mathematics
- Business Ethics and Society
- Civil War and Reconstruction
- Computing and Information Technology
- Criminal Justice
- Environmental Science
- Ethics in America
- Ethics in Technology
- Foundations of Education
- Fundamentals of College Algebra
- Fundamentals of Counseling
- Fundamentals of Cybersecurity
- General Anthropology
- Health and Human Development
- History of the Soviet Union
- Human Resource Management

- Introduction to Business
- Introduction to Geography
- Introduction to Geology
- Introduction to Law Enforcement
- Introduction to World Religions
- Lifespan Developmental Psychology
- Math for Liberal Arts
- Management Information Systems
- Money and Banking
- Organizational Behavior
- Personal Finance
- Principles of Advanced English Composition
- Principles of Finance
- Principles of Public Speaking
- Principles of Statistics
- Principles of Supervision
- Substance Abuse
- Technical Writing

Like what you see? Get unlimited access to Peterson's full catalog of DSST practice tests, instructional videos, flashcards, and more at **www.petersons.com/testprep/dsst.**

Chapter 1

All About the DSST® Exam

WHAT IS DSST®?

Previously known as the DANTES Subject Standardized Tests, the DSST program provides the opportunity for individuals to earn college credit for what they have learned outside of the traditional classroom. Accepted or administered at more than 1,500 colleges and universities nationwide and approved by the American Council on Education (ACE), the DSST program enables individuals to use the knowledge they have acquired outside the classroom to accomplish their educational and professional goals.

WHY TAKE A DSST® EXAM?

DSST exams offer a way for you to save both time and money in your quest for a college education. Why enroll in a college course in a subject you already understand? For more than 30 years, the DSST program has offered the perfect solution for individuals who are knowledgeable in a specific subject and want to save both time and money. A passing score on a DSST exam provides physical evidence to universities of proficiency in a specific subject. More than 1,500 accredited and respected colleges and universities across the nation award undergraduate credit for passing scores on DSST exams. With the DSST program, individuals can shave months off the time it takes to earn a degree.

The DSST program offers numerous advantages for individuals in all stages of their educational development:

- Adult learners
- College students
- Military personnel

Adult learners desiring college degrees face unique circumstances—demanding work schedules, family responsibilities, and tight budgets. Yet adult learners also have years of valuable work experience that can frequently be applied toward a degree through the DSST program. For example, adult learners with on-the-job experience in business and management might be able to skip the Business 101 courses if they earn passing marks on DSST exams such as Introduction to Business and Principles of Supervision.

Adult learners can put their prior learning into action and move forward with more advanced course work. Adults who have never enrolled in a college course may feel a little uncertain about their abilities. If this describes your situation, then sign up for a DSST exam and see how you do. A passing score may be the boost you need to realize your dream of earning a degree. With family and work commitments, adult learners often feel they lack the time to attend college. The DSST program provides adult learners with the unique opportunity to work toward college degrees without the time constraints of semester-long course work. DSST exams take two hours or less to complete. In one weekend, you could earn credit for multiple college courses.

The DSST exams also benefit students who are already enrolled in a college or university. With college tuition costs on the rise, most students face financial challenges. The fee for each DSST exam starts at $100 (plus administration fees charged by some testing facilities)—significantly less than the $750 average cost of a 3-hour college class. Maximize tuition assistance by taking DSST exams for introductory or mandatory course work. Once you earn a passing score on a DSST exam, you are free to move on to higher-level course work in that subject matter, take desired electives, or focus on courses in a chosen major.

Not only do college students and adult learners profit from DSST exams, but military personnel reap the benefits as well. If you are a member of the armed services at home or abroad, you can initiate your post-military career by taking DSST exams in areas with which you have experience. Military personnel can gain credit anywhere in the world, thanks to the fact that almost all of the tests are available through the internet at designated testing locations. DSST testing facilities are located at more than 500 military installations, so service members on active duty can get a jump-start on a post-military career with the DSST program. As an additional incentive, DANTES (Defense Activity for Non-Traditional Education Support) provides funding for DSST test fees for eligible members of the military.

More than 30 subject-matter tests are available in the fields of Business, Humanities, Math, Physical Science, Social Sciences, and Technology.

Available DSST® Exams

Business	Social Sciences
Business Ethics and Society	A History of the Vietnam War
Business Mathematics	Art of the Western World
Computing and Information Technology	Criminal Justice
Human Resource Management	Foundations of Education
Introduction to Business	Fundamentals of Counseling
Management Information Systems	General Anthropology
Money and Banking	History of the Soviet Union
Organizational Behavior	Introduction to Geography
Personal Finance	Introduction to Law Enforcement
Principles of Finance	Lifespan Developmental Psychology
Principles of Supervision	Substance Abuse
	The Civil War and Reconstruction
Humanities	**Physical Sciences**
Ethics in America	Astronomy
Introduction to World Religions	Environmental Science
Principles of Advanced English Composition	Health and Human Development
	Introduction to Geology
Principles of Public Speaking	
Math	**Technology**
Fundamentals of College Algebra	Ethics in Technology
Math for Liberal Arts	Fundamentals of Cybersecurity
Principles of Statistics	Technical Writing

As you can see from the table, the DSST program covers a wide variety of subjects. However, it is important to ask two questions before registering for a DSST exam.

1. Which universities or colleges award credit for passing DSST exams?
2. Which DSST exams are the most relevant to my desired degree and my experience?

Knowing which universities offer DSST credit is important. In all likelihood, a college in your area awards credit for DSST exams, but find out before taking an exam by contacting the university directly. Then review the list of DSST exams to determine which ones are most relevant to the degree you are seeking and to your base of knowledge. Schedule an appointment with your college adviser to determine which exams best fit your degree program and which college courses the DSST exams can replace. Advisers should also be able to tell you the minimum score required on the DSST exam to receive university credit.

DSST® TEST CENTERS

You can find DSST testing locations in community colleges and universities across the country. Check the DSST website (**www.getcollegecredit.com**) for a location near you or contact your local college or university to find out if the school administers DSST exams. Keep in mind that some universities and colleges administer DSST exams only to enrolled students.

DSST testing is available to men and women in the armed services at more than 500 military installations around the world. Can't get to a testing facility? Remote proctoring is now available for servicemembers. Check the DSST website for more details.

HOW TO REGISTER FOR A DSST® EXAM

Once you have located a nearby DSST testing facility, you need to contact the testing center to find out the exam administration schedule. Many centers are set up to administer tests via the internet, while others use printed materials. Almost all DSST exams are available as online tests, but the method used depends on the testing center. The cost for each DSST exam starts at $100, and many testing locations charge a fee to cover their costs for administering the tests. Credit cards are the only accepted payment method for taking online DSST exams. Credit card, certified check, and money order are acceptable payment methods for paper-and-pencil tests.

Test takers are allotted two score reports—one mailed to them and another mailed to a designated college or university, if requested. Online tests generate unofficial scores at the end of the test session, while individuals taking paper tests must wait four to six weeks for score reports.

PREPARING FOR A DSST® EXAM

Even though you are knowledgeable in a certain subject matter, you should still prepare for the test to ensure you achieve the highest score possible.

The first step in studying for a DSST exam is to find out what will be on the specific test you have chosen. Information regarding test content is located on the DSST fact sheets, which can be downloaded at no cost from www. getcollegecredit.com. Each fact sheet outlines the topics covered on a subject-matter test, as well as the approximate percentage assigned to each topic. For example, questions on the Business Ethics and Society exam are distributed in the following way: The Importance of Business Ethics – 7%, Moral Philosophies and Business Ethics – 9%, Corporations and Stakeholders – 13%, Social Responsibilities of a Business – 10%, Regulation of Business – 9%, Employer-Employee Relations – 20%, Ethics of Information – 16%, and Business Ethics in a Global Economy – 16%.

In addition to the breakdown of topics on a DSST exam, the fact sheet also lists recommended reference materials. If you do not own the recommended books, then check college bookstores. Avoid paying high prices for new textbooks by looking online for used textbooks. Don't panic if you are unable to locate a specific textbook listed on the fact sheet; the textbooks are merely recommendations. Instead, search for comparable books used in university courses on the specific subject. Current editions are ideal, and it is a good idea to use at least two references when studying for a DSST exam. Of course, the subject matter provided in this book will be a sufficient review for most test takers. However, if you need additional information, then it is a good idea to have some of the reference materials at your disposal when preparing for a DSST exam.

Fact sheets include other useful information in addition to a list of reference materials and topics. Each fact sheet includes subject-specific sample questions like those you will encounter on the DSST exam. The sample questions provide an idea of the types of questions you can expect on the exam. Test questions are multiple-choice with one correct answer and three incorrect choices.

The fact sheet also includes information about the number of credit hours ACE has recommended be awarded by colleges for a passing DSST exam score. However, you should keep in mind that not all universities and colleges adhere to the ACE recommendation for DSST credit hours. Some institutions require DSST exam scores higher than the minimum score recommended by ACE. Once you have acquired appropriate reference materials and you have the outline provided on the fact sheet, you are ready to start studying, which is where this book can help.

TEST DAY

After reviewing the material and taking practice tests, you are finally ready to take your DSST exam. Follow these tips for a successful test day experience.

1. **Arrive on time.** Not only is it courteous to arrive on time to the DSST testing facility, but it also allows plenty of time for you to take care of check-in procedures and settle into your surroundings.
2. **Bring identification.** DSST test facilities require that candidates bring a valid government-issued identification card with a current photo and signature. Acceptable forms of identification include a current driver's license, passport, military identification card, or state-issued identification card. Individuals who fail to bring proper identification to the DSST testing facility will not be allowed to take an exam.
3. **Bring the right supplies.** If your exam requires the use of a calculator, you may bring a calculator that meets the specifications. For paper-based exams, you may also bring No. 2 pencils with an eraser and black ballpoint pens. Regardless of the exam methodology, you are NOT allowed to bring reference or study materials, scratch paper, or electronics such as cell phones, personal handheld devices, cameras, alarm wrist watches, or recording devices to the testing center.
4. **Take the test.** During the exam, take the time to read each question-and-answer option carefully. Eliminate the choices you know are incorrect to narrow the number of potential answers. If a question completely stumps you, take an educated guess and move on—remember that DSSTs are timed; you will have 2 hours to take the exam.

With the proper preparation, DSST exams will save you both time and money. So join the thousands of people who have already reaped the benefits of DSST exams and move closer than ever to your college degree.

BUSINESS ETHICS AND SOCIETY EXAM FACTS

The *DSST® Business Ethics and Society* exam consists of 100 multiple-choice questions that cover material commonly found in a college-level business ethics and society course, including the importance of business ethics, moral philosophies and business ethics, social responsibilities of a business, employer-employee relations, and business ethics in a global economy.

Area or Course Equivalent: Ethics & Society
Level: Lower-level baccalaureate
Amount of Credit: 3 Semester Hours
Minimum Score: 400
Source: https://getcollegecredit.com/wp-content/uploads/2021/12/BusinessEthicsAndSociety.pdf

I. **The Importance of Business Ethics – 7%**

    a. Fundamentals of business ethics—i.e., profit–motive

    b. Issues raised by business scandals, fraud, and insider trading

    c. Ethical leadership

II. **Moral Philosophies and Business Ethics – 9%**

    a. Moral development

    b. Philosophies—e.g., egoism, relativism, utilitarianism, etc.

III. **Corporations and Stakeholders – 13%**

    a. Relationship with stockholders

    b. Relationship with employees

    c. Corporations and consumers

    d. The corporation within the community and the public good

IV. **Social Responsibilities of a Business – 10%**

    a. Moral and ethical stances

    b. Individual responsibilities within a business

    c. Global responsibilities of a business

    d. Sustainable business growth and environmental responsibility

V. **Regulation of Business – 9%**

    a. Theoretical issues

    b. Business and politics—i.e., political contributions, conflicts of interest, etc.

    c. Governmental control over business activities

VI. **Employer-Employee Relations – 20%**

   a. Confidentiality and whistleblowing

   b. Discrimination and affirmative action

   c. Sexual harassment

   d. Duties of corporate officers—i.e., workplace safety, etc.

   e. Labor relations—i.e., unions, at-will, etc.

VII. **Ethics of Information – 16%**

   a. Marketing and advertising

   b. Corporate espionage and cybersecurity

   c. Privacy issues/concerns

   d. Control of proprietary information

   e. Information technology regulations

VIII. **Business Ethics in a Global Economy – 16%**

   a. Corporate citizenship

   b. Ethics in transnational corporations

   c. Outsourcing and offshoring

   d. Ethical standards in different countries

   e. Fair trade laws and standards (e.g., WTO, NAFTA, etc.)

Chapter 2

Business Ethics and Society Diagnostic Test

DIAGNOSTIC TEST ANSWER SHEET

1. Ⓐ Ⓑ Ⓒ Ⓓ

2. Ⓐ Ⓑ Ⓒ Ⓓ

3. Ⓐ Ⓑ Ⓒ Ⓓ

4. Ⓐ Ⓑ Ⓒ Ⓓ

5. Ⓐ Ⓑ Ⓒ Ⓓ

6. Ⓐ Ⓑ Ⓒ Ⓓ

7. Ⓐ Ⓑ Ⓒ Ⓓ

8. Ⓐ Ⓑ Ⓒ Ⓓ

9. Ⓐ Ⓑ Ⓒ Ⓓ

10. Ⓐ Ⓑ Ⓒ Ⓓ

11. Ⓐ Ⓑ Ⓒ Ⓓ

12. Ⓐ Ⓑ Ⓒ Ⓓ

13. Ⓐ Ⓑ Ⓒ Ⓓ

14. Ⓐ Ⓑ Ⓒ Ⓓ

15. Ⓐ Ⓑ Ⓒ Ⓓ

16. Ⓐ Ⓑ Ⓒ Ⓓ

17. Ⓐ Ⓑ Ⓒ Ⓓ

18. Ⓐ Ⓑ Ⓒ Ⓓ

19. Ⓐ Ⓑ Ⓒ Ⓓ

20. Ⓐ Ⓑ Ⓒ Ⓓ

BUSINESS ETHICS AND SOCIETY DIAGNOSTIC TEST
24 minutes—20 questions

Directions: Carefully read each of the following 20 questions. Choose the best answer to each question and fill in the corresponding circle on the answer sheet. The Answer Key and Explanations can be found following this Diagnostic Test.

1. Which of the following philosophies is based on a version of consequential ethics?

   A. Ethical relativism
   B. Utilitarianism
   C. Virtue ethics
   D. Deontological theory

2. What is it called when an employee of one company has a huge investment in another business that is bidding for a contract with the employee's place of business?

   A. Divestiture
   B. Affirmative action
   C. Disclosure duty
   D. Conflict of interest

3. The basic rights to owning property, freedom of choice, fair competition, and profits are found under which economic system?

   A. Communistic enterprise system
   B. Socialistic enterprise system
   C. Private enterprise system
   D. Public enterprise system

4. What are the key responsibilities that companies have to their employees?

   I. Providing workplace safety
   II. Protection from discrimination
   III. Equal opportunities on the job

   A. I and II only.
   B. I and III only.
   C. II and III only.
   D. I, II, and II.

5. Which of the following is a controversial practice of raising prices on commonly needed items to cover associated costs for researching new products?

A. Pricing strategy
B. Skimming
C. Shilling
D. Target pricing

6. When it comes to social responsibility of a business, what characteristic is most important for employees to have?

A. Loyalty
B. Integrity
C. Fairness
D. Collaboration

7. Which of the following statements is true about outsourcing and offshoring?

A. Outsourcing involves using vendors in another country, and offshoring is about relocation of business processes within the same country.
B. Outsourcing involves using vendors in another country, and offshoring is about relocation of business processes outside of the country.
C. Outsourcing involves using vendors for goods previously handled in-house or in-country, and offshoring is about relocation of business processes outside of the country.
D. Outsourcing involves using vendors for goods previously handled in-house, and offshoring is about relocation of business processes outside of the country.

8. What morality is violated when a company spies on another company?

A. Virtue
B. Accountability
C. Justness
D. Respect

9. Which of the following would be a violation of a corporate officer's duty during the planning phase for a new building?

   A. The corporate officer does not use a contractor recommended
   by a board director due to cost factors.
   B. The corporate officer tells the contractor not to build a second
   escape route because of the added cost.
   C. The corporate officer tells the contractor to go with the small-
   est size offices that OSHA allows.
   D. The corporate officer does not incorporate the ideas put forth
   by employees because they do not think the employees know
   enough to make recommendations.

10. Adam Smith is often identified as the father of capitalism because
of his economic theory based on the idea that

   A. an economy is best regulated by the invisible hand of
   competition.
   B. individuals implicitly agree to live according to a society's rules
   simply by the fact of remaining within that society.
   C. individuals should act in accordance with what is in one's own
   self-interest.
   D. one's morality is in alignment with one's culture.

11. Which of the following federal acts stiffened the penalties placed
on employers who intentionally discriminate on the basis of an
employee's disability?

   A. Title VII of the Civil Rights Act of 1964
   B. Vocational Rehabilitation Act of 1973
   C. American with Disabilities Act of 1990
   D. Genetic Information Nondiscrimination Act of 2008

12. What is the foundation for the idea behind global corporate
citizenship?

   A. Thomas Hobbes' Social Contract Theory
   B. Kohlberg's Stages of Moral Development
   C. Adam Smith's Invisible Hand Theory
   D. Immanuel Kant's Moral Theory

13. *Quid pro quo* is the term used to describe a type of

A. sexual harassment in which an employee feels hassled or degraded because of unwelcome flirting, lewd comments, or obscene jokes.

B. sexual harassment in which an employee is pressured to comply with unwelcome advances in return for job security.

C. discrimination in which a job applicant is asked for a donation in return for getting the job.

D. discrimination in which an older worker is dismissed in favor of hiring a younger employee.

14. Which of the following is NOT a right of a shareholder?

A. Inspecting financial statements

B. Producing materially accurate representations of financial position

C. Dividends

D. Voting for board of directors

15. What do transnational corporations contribute to in addition to global economics?

A. Political diversity

B. Employment growth

C. Removal of trade restrictions

D. Cultural diversity

16. Which of the following is an illegal and unethical form of advertisement?

A. Cause advertising

B. Sale of hazardous products with adequate disclosure

C. Written misrepresentation of what a product does

D. Hidden fees

17. How can a company try to protect a consumer's private information stored online?

A. Cybersecurity system

B. Terms of agreement

C. Written policies

D. Marketing contracts

18. When it comes to sustainability, corporations are NOT responsible for which of the following?

A. The environment
B. The communities in which they operate
C. The political climate
D. Profit growth

19. What is the term for the negotiation process between management of a company and union representatives?

A. Collective bargaining
B. Arbitration
C. Mediation
D. Strike

20. When a government steps in to enact laws to ensure fair competition and to ensure that the economic markets run effectively, this is known as what type of regulation?

A. Business regulation
B. Laissez faire regulation
C. Deregulation
D. Government compliance regulation

ANSWER KEY AND EXPLANATIONS

1. B	**5.** B	**9.** B	**13.** B	**17.** A
2. D	**6.** B	**10.** A	**14.** B	**18.** C
3. C	**7.** C	**11.** C	**15.** D	**19.** A
4. D	**8.** C	**12.** D	**16.** C	**20.** D

1. **The correct answer is B.** Utilitarianism derives from the theory that moral behavior is based upon the idea that the consequences of an action determine whether the action is right or wrong. Ethical relativism (choice A) is based on the idea that society norms determine what is morally right. For this reason, what is right in one society may be wrong in another. Virtue ethics (choice C) looks at the moral character of the person rather than the action taken. If the person is acting in accordance with one's belief of right, then the action is morally right. Deontological theory (choice D) is based on the idea that the morality of the action is all that matters—not its consequences.

2. **The correct answer is D.** A conflict of interest exists when an individual's interests have the potential of harming another's. In this example, the employee may place pressure on the company to hire the other company with which they have an invested interest in. Divestiture (choice A) deals with having investments in different types of accounts. Affirmative action (choice B) deals with hiring and promotion activities. Duty to disclose (choice C) is the action individuals should take when they have a conflict of interest.

3. **The correct answer is C.** A private enterprise system provides for rights to owning property, freedom of choice, fair competition, and profits. A communistic system (choice A) does not allow ownership of property or freedom of choice, which also rules out competition. In socialism (choice B), private ownership of property is not allowed for most major industries. Public ownership (choice D) indicates government ownership rather than private ownership.

4. **The correct answer is D.** Companies are responsible for providing employees with the assurance of workplace safety, protection from discrimination, and equal opportunities on the job.

5. **The correct answer is B.** Skimming is a pricing strategy that allows companies to recuperate some of their research costs through charging a higher price to the consumer. Pharmaceutical companies have come under fire for a type of medical skimming, where they raise prices on commonly needed drugs in order to cover the associated costs for researching new drugs. Ethical challenges occur when skimming is paired with advertising that is not truthful or when a manufacturer charges a higher price because consumers want a product and there is little to no competition.

6. **The correct answer is B.** For a business to be socially responsible, it is most important for employees to have integrity. With integrity, employees will be honest in what they do and how they do it, ensuring the company responds ethically to its social responsibilities. While loyalty (choice A) is good for an employee to have, loyalty at the expense of truth can result in an employee not disclosing unethical behavior. Fairness (choice C) is based on individual morality. What one employee might see as fair may not be the same for another employee. Collaboration (choice D) can be good or bad, depending on the result of the union.

7. **The correct answer is C.** Outsourcing does not necessarily mean that a business is outsourcing its processes to another country. Outsourcing can involve choosing a vendor instead of producing within the company, but said vendors can be either in the same country as the business or in another country. Offshoring always involves using firms outside of the country in which the company resides. Choices A and B incorrectly define outsourcing as only occurring in another country. Choice A also falsely says offshoring is relocation within the same country. Choice D incorrectly defines outsourcing as only dealing with previously handled in-house processes, rather than also including processes that were previously handled by another company in-country.

8. **The correct answer is C.** Justness involves being fair. When one company spies on another, the spying company is not being fair to the other company that has already spent the effort and money to develop a new or improved product or process. *Virtue* (choice A) is another word for *morality*. Accountability (choice B) deals with responsibility. Respect (choice D) deals with admiration of another.

9. **The correct answer is B.** A corporate officer has a moral duty to maintain workplace safety. Cost should not be a factor in workplace safety, and a second escape route is routine for safety purposes. Choice A is incorrect because while a board of directors sets overall policy and authorizes major transactions, it does not get involved in the detailed work of obtaining bids. Choice C is incorrect because OSHA sets safety standards; it does not matter if the officer goes with the minimum requirements. While an officer should be respectful to employees and their opinions, choice D is not the best answer because an officer's duty involves doing what they think is in the best interest of the company.

10. **The correct answer is A.** Adam Smith's Invisible Hand Theory centers on the idea of competition as the basis for capitalism. Choice B describes Thomas Hobbes' societal contract. Choice C describes ethical egoism. Choice D describes the theory of ethical relativism.

11. **The correct answer is C.** The American with Disabilities Act of 1990 prohibits discrimination against the disabled in regard to public accommodations, transportation, and telecommunications. The act also increased the penalties associated with employers who intentionally discriminate on the basis of an employee's disability. Title VII of the Civil Rights Act of 1964 (choice A) made discrimination on the basis of race, color, religion, sex, or national origin illegal, but did not include disability. The Vocational Rehabilitation Act of 1973 (choice B) requires government contractors and subcontractors to take affirmative action to employ and promote qualified disabled individuals. The Genetic Information Nondiscrimination Act of 2008 (choice D) makes it illegal to discriminate on the basis of one's genetic information.

12. **The correct answer is D.** According to Kant's Moral Theory, consequences do not determine whether an action is moral or not; rather, morality is determined by whether or not the action meets or fulfills one's duty. Global corporate citizenship is based on the idea that global responsibility is moral as it fulfills one's duty to the world. Hobbes' theory (choice A) is based on the idea of belonging to one society and acting in accordance with that society's morals and norms rather than a worldwide good. Kohlberg's theory (choice B) categorized six stages of moral development with the highest stage never obtainable. Smith's theory (choice C) is an economic theory regarding competition.

13. **The correct answer is B.** *Quid pro quo* is Latin for "something for something." In this type of sexual harassment, the first something is sexual favors, and the second something is keeping a job. Choice A is a different type of sexual harassment that occurs in a hostile work environment, where the work atmosphere is made uncomfortable but job security is not threatened. Choice C represents a form of bribery. Choice D is age discrimination.

14. **The correct answer is B.** Shareholders have the right to inspect financial statements, the right to dividends, and the right to vote for board members. The executives of a corporation have a duty to the shareholders to produce materially accurate representations of financial position.

15. **The correct answer is D.** Transnational corporations introduce their culture to employees in other countries and vice-versa. While transnational corporations have a political influence, choice A is not the best answer because political diversity is not necessarily part of the mix. While employment growth (choice B) and removal of trade restrictions (choice C) are two factors that are a part of global economics, these answers are incorrect because the question is asking what *additional* contribution is made by such companies, which is cultural diversity.

16. **The correct answer is C.** It is both illegal and unethical to misrepresent a product. Cause advertising (choice A) promotes a specific viewpoint on a public issue as a way to influence opinion. As long as that promotion does not misrepresent, it is perfectly legal and ethical. Choice B is incorrect because it is legal to sell a dangerous product, such as fireworks, as long as there is full disclosure to ensure awareness of danger. Choice D is incorrect because it is both illegal and unethical to have hidden fees.

17. **The correct answer is A.** A cybersecurity system tries to protect a company's data, which includes consumers' private information. Terms of agreement (choice B) can include the company's right to sell or share consumer information. Written policies (choice C) are the same as terms of agreements. Marketing contracts (choice D) give an outside company the rights to the information on the seller's website, which includes consumers' private information.

18. **The correct answer is C.** While corporations try to influence governments through lobbying, they are not responsible for sustaining a political climate. Choices A, B, and D represent the three factors that companies have a social responsibility and corporate duty to sustain—the planet, people, and profits.

19. **The correct answer is A.** Collective bargaining is the process that occurs whenever a union contract is due to expire and a new contract is being drawn up. Arbitration (choice B) is what occurs when there is a particular grievance against the company by an individual or multiple union members. Mediation (choice C) is the same as arbitration in that it deals with a grievance. A strike (choice D) is what union members do when the collective bargaining process fails.

20. **The correct answer is D.** Governments regulate business in the core areas of advertising, labor, environmental impact, privacy, and health and safety. Because businesses are regulated by profit, governments step in to protect investors, employees, and the general public. The laws enacted on business activities are known as government compliance regulations.

DIAGNOSTIC TEST ASSESSMENT GRID

Now that you've completed the diagnostic test and read through the answer explanations, you can use your results to target your studying. Find the question numbers from the diagnostic test that you answered incorrectly and highlight or circle them below. Then focus extra attention on the sections dealing with those topics.

Business Ethics and Society		
Content Area	**Topic**	**Question #**
The importance of Business Ethics	• Fundamentals of business ethics—i.e., profit-motive • Issues raised by business scandals, fraud, and insider trading • Ethical leadership	3
Moral Philosophies and Business Ethics	• Moral development • Philosophies—e.g., egotism, relativism, utilitarianism, etc.	1, 10
Corporations and Stakeholders	• Relationship with stockholders • Relationship with employees • Corporations and consumers • The corporation within the community and the public good	4, 14, 16
Social Responsibilities of a Business	• Moral and ethical standards • Individual responsibilities within a business • Global responsibilities of a business • Sustainable business growth and environmental responsibility	6, 18
Regulation of Business	• Theoretical issues • Business and politics—i.e., political contributions, conflicts of interest, etc. • Governmental control over business activities	2, 20

Content Area	Topic	Question #
Employer-Employee Relations	• Confidentiality and whistleblowing • Discrimination and affirmative action • Sexual harassment • Duties of corporate officers—i.e., workplace safety, etc. • Labor relations—i.e., unions, at-will, etc.	9, 11, 13, 19
Ethics of Information and Information Technology	• Marketing and advertising • Corporate espionage and cybersecurity • Privacy issues/concerns • Control of proprietary information • Information technology regulations	5, 8, 17
Business Ethics in a Global Economy	• Corporate citizenship • Ethics in transnational corporations • Outsourcing and off-shoring • Ethical standards in different countries • Fair trade laws and standards—e.g., WTO, NAFTA, etc.	7, 12, 15

Chapter 3

Business Ethics and Society Subject Review

OVERVIEW

- The Importance of Business Ethics
- Moral Philosophies and Business Ethics
- Corporations and Stakeholders
- Social Responsibilities of a Business
- Regulation of Business
- Employer-Employee Relations
- Ethics of Information
- Business Ethics in a Global Economy
- Summing It Up

THE IMPORTANCE OF BUSINESS ETHICS

Business ethics, also called **business morals**, is the standards of conduct and values governing decision-making and actions in the business environment. This section will explore the fundamentals of business ethics, ethical issues raised by the occurrence of scandals, fraud, and insider trading, and the importance of ethical leadership. Approximately seven percent of the questions on the DSST exam will cover this topic.

Fundamentals of Business Ethics

Prior to 1760, farming was the main business industry. In general, individuals supervised themselves and were primarily interested in producing enough crops to survive. If more could be produced, all the better. The Industrial Revolution is credited with shifting the workforce into factories. With this change, new challenges arose. Manufacturing required a new set of skills, among which was the management of others. Companies often had multiple owners, each of whom had a stake in these factories. Because of the investment these owners made in their businesses, profit became a main driving force.

As this profit-motive became more of a focal point for businesses, questions arose regarding the treatment of employees and the rights of business owners and their stakeholders. Governments began regulating businesses as the ethics of the profit-motive came into question. It became clear that all companies, no matter what their size, had something in common—an economic impact on the country in which they were located and an ability to meet the wants and needs of society.

Various economic systems evolved because of differing opinions as to whom should own and operate businesses. Three basic economic systems developed as a result: the **free-enterprise system**, **communism**, and **socialism**.

Types of Government Economic Systems

System Name	Freedom of Choice	Fair Competition	Who Operates	Distribution of Profits
Free-Enterprise System	Yes	Strongly encouraged	Private enterprise	Goes to business owners
Communism	No	None	Government	Government
Socialism	Some	Not truly supported	Mostly government	Government

NOTE: Adam Smith is identified as the father of capitalism, synonymous with free enterprise, because of his economic theory based on the idea that an economy is best regulated by the *invisible hand* of competition.

Issues Raised by Business Scandals, Fraud, and Insider Trading

On average, US corporations lose approximately 5% of their revenues every year in undetected frauds, per the Association of Certified Fraud Examiners. Undetected fraud impacts not only a company's financial statements, but its reputation as well. An "underperforming" company may have more serious issues to deal with besides its performance.

Financial statement fraud costs companies more than any other type of fraud because its effects are so far-reaching. There are shorter-term, measurable costs associated with discovering a fraud that include legal fees, fines, and penalties. Losing the trust of investors and consumers has a much larger, longer lasting effect that is often difficult to quantify. The following table lists two types of fraud that can result in financial statement misstatements.

Two Types of Financial Statement Fraud

Type of Unethical Behavior	Who Is Acting as Such	Who Is Unaware until Too Late
Misrepresenting financial statements	Corporation officers	Stockholders
Misappropriation of assets	General employees	Corporate officers

Improper revenue recognition is the most common type of misrepresentation found on financial information, specifically financial statements. This includes improper timing of revenue recognition, fictitious revenues, inflated income due to one-time gains, nonrecognition of liabilities, improper recognition of expenses, and improper cash flow presentation. This type of fraud is usually committed by senior management or officers that have access to high-level financial information.

Misappropriation of assets is the theft of an entity's assets for personal gain. This happens when trusted people within an organization abuse their authority and power to steal company or client assets through fraudulent activities.

Asset Misappropriation Activities

Corporate Asset Fraud	• Billing, payroll, or expense reimbursement fraud • Check tampering • Misuse or theft of assets • Skimming
Client Asset Fraud	• Embezzlement • Larceny • Ponzi schemes

Any individual who has an opportunity, a motive, and a rationalization of the act can misappropriate assets. Corporate asset fraud is usually attributed to unethical lower-level employees, managers, or individuals who work in the accounting department. Client asset fraud generally occurs at a higher level.

Insider trading involves individuals who have *inside* information that provides them with knowledge ahead of time of business dealings that might impact the value of company stock. When individuals use this information to personally gain by either buying up stock while the price is still low or selling stock while the price is still high, they are committing insider trading. Insider trading gives these individuals a huge edge over other stockholders in the company.

The moral issue in such activity is the unfairness to other stockholders who, like the inside trader, are owners of the corporation. In response to this ethical issue, government legislatures stepped in and created the **Securities and Exchange Act of 1934**. This act prevented corporate officers, directors, and shareholders who own 10% or more of stock who buy and sell their stock within six months from keeping the proceeds. Such proceeds must go back to the company.

Scandals impact more than just a company's bottom line. They bring unethical conduct into the spotlight, highlighting a lack of integrity and honest leadership. In 2018, Elon Musk, the CEO of Tesla, made a public claim on Twitter that he was taking the company private, and that he had secured the funds to do so. By making the claim in such a public manner, Musk was trying to manipulate the market by providing false information to drive the stock price higher. The SEC sued, and Musk settled with the SEC, stepping temporarily down from his position in the company and agreeing to limitations on his Twitter usage. However, this highly publicized scandal spurred much discussion over the importance of ethical leadership and how companies could foster a better environment.

Ethical Leadership

An ethical atmosphere in the workplace starts with the development of a corporate values statement that includes the values of integrity, loyalty, and honesty. However, for these values to be accepted in the workplace, leadership must demonstrate their commitment to the value statement not only through their actions, but through the cultivation of a work culture that values its employees. If leadership does not display ethical behavior, then employees are less likely to act ethically.

MORAL PHILOSOPHIES AND BUSINESS ETHICS

This section will explore moral development and philosophies and their connection to business ethics. Approximately nine percent of the questions on the DSST exam cover this topic.

Moral Development

Many say that **morals** are based upon one's upbringing and religious beliefs. However, not all individuals end up sharing the same beliefs as the generation that raised them. Some individuals mature into higher levels of morality than others do. What causes this change?

Cognitive disequilibrium occurs when an individual is faced with conflicting views. To develop moral growth, this person must realize that differences exist and work through how to deal with those differences. For example, someone might grow up in a household with a religious background that believes in capital punishment. If that person is never confronted with a situation in which they see a conflict with such punishment, then that individual will likely remain at the same stage of morality regarding this belief. However, if that individual discovers that an innocent person has died from capital punishment, they will probably question the morality of the belief and the law. It helps to keep in mind that morality is a fluid or dynamic process.

In addition to cognitive disequilibrium, an individual cannot make an ethical decision if they are unable to identify an ethical situation. A person cannot react if they are unaware of a moral dilemma. Thus, moral development is based upon both cognitive disequilibrium and moral sensitivity.

Psychologist **Lawrence Kohlberg** identified that individuals typically develop moral standards in six different stages that can be grouped into three different levels of development. These stages are not dependent upon the ethical background a person has experienced.

Kohlberg's Theory of Moral Development

Stage	Moral Standard	Level of Moral Development
1	Obedience and Punishment	Pre-conventional
2	Individualism and Exchange	
3	Good Interpersonal Relationships	Conventional
4	Maintaining Social Order	
5	Social Contract and Individual Rights	Post-conventional
6	Universal Principals	

In the **pre-conventional level of moral development**, an individual's choice as to whether to behave is based solely upon consequences to one-self. In Stage 1, an individual acts to avoid punishment and concludes that the greater the punishment, the worse the behavior must be. In Stage 2, individuals recognize that there may be more than one "right" view. In other words, different people have different viewpoints.

At the **conventional level**, morality turns to societal and personal relationships. An individual behaves according to what is necessary to have a positive relationship or be a good person. Stage 3 development is oriented toward behaving to avoid disapproval from others, which goes beyond personal approval to outside approval. In other words, this stage values the approval of others. In Stage 4, while behavior is still dictated by outside forces—laws and other types of guidelines—a person acts to do what is believed to be the "right" thing. A good example of this stage in action is when people feel as though they are morally correct because they found a loophole in a rule, and no one chastises them for the behavior. The law, as written, was obeyed, and the action did not change anyone's opinion of the loophole finder.

At the **post-conventional level**, morality becomes more abstract and values-based. In Stage 5, orientation to social contracts leads one to understand that there are many different societies with very different norms and values that should be respected. While rules may exist for the good of the greatest number, there may be times when these rules will work against the interest of certain individuals. Finally, in Stage 6, abstract reasoning leads to behavior so entrenched in the morals of equality of justice that it becomes one's duty to rebuke unjust laws no matter what the cost. Kohlberg believed that very few people reached this final stage.

According to research in the workplace, most people are at the conventional level of stage 4. This research makes sense as it coincides with **Maslow's hierarchy of needs**. According to Maslow's theory, everyone first has the physiological needs for basic survival: food, shelter, etc. The next level of need is one of safety, followed by the need for social belongingness. Esteem needs and self-actualization needs round out the hierarchy. Like Kohlberg's Stage 4, esteem needs are based on personal needs influenced by outside forces, such as being accepted by those in authority.

Philosophies

Debates about how moral decisions are made or the proper basis for making a moral decision have been occurring for centuries. The first philosophical theories on this issue were based on the idea that all mankind is entitled to certain rights. Basically, there are two types of rights: (1) natural rights and (2) those rights founded on covenants. Many of these rights are based upon freedoms such as free speech, freedom to consent, and freedom from oppression.

Thomas Hobbes is considered to be one of the founders of modern political philosophy. According to Hobbes, a **social contract** is a framework for how individuals should behave in accordance with laws and certain expectations. He believed that the natural state of mankind (i.e., the "state of nature") is a state of war of one man against another, as man is selfish and brutish. Social contracts evolved to create societal protections. There is a need for a mutual transferring of this right when living in a society.

How is Hobbes' social contract theory relevant to business today? By virtue of accepting a job offer, an employee is giving up certain individualistic behaviors and rights in agreement to follow the company's rules and processes. This type of contract is called a **psychological contract**. Like the social contract, the psychological contract is often implicit, but there are cases in which it is explicit, such as in formal employment agreements. These contracts include informal arrangements, mutual beliefs, common ground, and perceptions between the employer and the employee. It is a dynamic arrangement in that expectations evolve over time based upon communications between the employer and employee. Examples of some basic expectations in a psychological contract include the employer expecting the employee to be at work on time, and the employee expecting to get paid by the employer on time.

Hobbes' social contract theory was based on his belief that everyone has a right to everything in nature. However, there would be total chaos if individuals were allowed to help themselves to everything. In addition to living in a society and obeying that society's rules, what else supports a collective well-being? We know that new laws are created every day, so what helps the majority to act morally in-between the enactment of laws? The answer is virtue.

A **virtue** is a characteristic that supports morality and a collective well-being. Aristotle identified many different virtues, including justice, honesty, integrity, loyalty, and courage. A good example of virtues supporting moral decision-making can be seen in the public accounting profession. When a public accountant is honest and has the courage to not succumb to pressure about the opinion they provide on a company's financial statements, the right of shareholders to know the truth is supported.

Various philosophers have found that morality is also based on other factors. The three broad categories of ethical theory are **rights**, **consequentiality**, and **deontology**.

Ethical Theories

General Categorization	Specific Theory	Key Word(s) to Theory
Rights	Social contract	Societal rights
	Relativism	Societal norms and values
Consequentiality	Egoism	Self-interest
	Utilitarianism	Greatest number
Deontology	Kantian	Duty

Rights includes the major offshoot of ethical relativism. **Relativism** is based on the idea that societal norms determine what is morally right. Under relativism, nothing is ever always right or always wrong. Right or wrong are subjective, depending on the norms of the period or the values of a particular society. An example of relativism at play in business would be an Egyptian retailer marking products at an outrageous price. According to relativism, this action is moral because the norm in Egyptian society is to bargain the price of all goods. Retailers know that they will not get their asking price because of the societal norm. An argument against relativism, however, is the fact that almost every culture has some form of the golden rule of doing unto others as you would have done unto you.

Consequentiality is based upon the idea that to be moral, a decision needs to be based upon the consequences of the chosen action. Several of the major theories stemming from this category of consequences include egoism and utilitarianism.

The theory of **egoism** explains that moral decisions are based on the consequences to one's own self. In this theory, self-interest is a virtue. Even though *egoism* and *egotistical* have the same root word, the egoism theory is not based on boastfulness and inappropriate pride. Instead, egoism helps guide one's moral decision. For example, egoists would believe that giving handouts instead of teaching people to be independent is degrading to those receiving the hand-out. It is not in the best interest of that individual to provide a handout as such action continues to make those receiving the handout dependent upon the generosity of others. Another example of egoism would be those who don't kill others because it is not in the individual's best interest to do so.

Unlike egoism, **utilitarianism** is based upon the idea of the greatest good. The consequences of an action determine whether the action is right or wrong. In other words, moral decisions are based upon the choice that makes the greatest number of people happy. The golden rule of doing unto others as you would have them do unto you is an example of utilitarianism. The platinum rule takes the golden rule to higher moral standard as it says do unto others as they would have done unto themselves.

Deontology stems from **Immanuel Kant's theory** that morality does not stem from consideration of consequences. Kant argued that moral behavior should not and is not led by a fear of punishment or belief in God. Basing moral behavior on these factors would indicate that anyone who is agnostic or atheist is immoral. According to Kant, morality is based on duty. Everyone has duties to others, and it is that duty that determines whether an action is right or wrong depending on whether that duty was fulfilled.

CORPORATIONS AND STAKEHOLDERS

This section will focus on corporations and stakeholders. Specifically, the relationships with stockholders, employees, consumers, and the responsibilities of a corporation within the community and the public good. Approximately 13 percent of the questions on the DSST exam cover this topic.

Relationship with Stockholders

Duty is key to moral business practices between corporations and their **stakeholders**. Stakeholders include shareholders, employees, customers, vendors, and the community at-large. In order to understand the duty that corporations have, one must first understand how corporations are owned. Individuals looking to invest in companies will buy stock in companies that look to be high performers. This stock gives the stock or shareholder a part ownership in the business.

There are two types of stock that give the shareholder different rights: preferred and common. **Preferred stock** usually costs more, but it gives preferred shareholders rights to receive dividends and assets from the corporation before the common shareholders. **Common stock** gives a shareholder voting rights to elect the board of directors. Thus, common shareholders have a duty, especially those with larger amounts of stock in the company, to review board candidates and to vote in favor of individuals with known integrity.

In return, the corporation, through the actions of its board of directors and corporate officers (e.g., CEO and CFO), has a **fiduciary duty** to both types of shareholders. A fiduciary duty means the corporate officers must act in a way that benefits the shareholder financially, rather than themselves. The aim is to align the goals of corporate officers with the shareholders. It is for this reason that corporate officers have such high compensation packages.

Rights of Shareholders and the Duties of a Corporation

Shareholders' Rights	Executive Duties to Shareholders
• Right to inspect financial statements	• Duty to produce materially accurate representation of financial position
• Right to dividends (return on investments)	• Duty to work for an appropriate return on shareholders' investments
• Right to vote for board of directors	• Duty to work towards fulfilling corporation's mission
	• Fiduciary duty to protect shareholders' assets

However, the existence of severance plans known as **golden parachutes** where benefits are given to an executive upon dismissal have brought to light an interesting ethical dilemma. In these plans, the corporate officer is being compensated for putting the shareholders' interests first. However, when the separation occurs at a time when the corporation is either not doing well or has failed, is it ethical for a corporate officer to be entitled to a golden parachute?

A **corporate charter** contains a company's bylaws, formal policy, and procedures for managing the business at a strategic level. These documents provide for the corporate governance of the business, making the expectations among corporate officers, shareholders, and corporate management clear. When a corporate charter is missing or has not been updated to align with changes that have occurred in the company, ethical issues ensue. In the early 2000s, when businesses such as WorldCom began taking over smaller companies, they failed to establish a common corporate governance over all their subsidiaries. As a result, fraudulent activities occurred, and stockholders suffered huge losses in their investments.

The **Sarbanes-Oxley Act of 2002** was enacted to address corporate accountability and help protect shareholders, employees, and the public from incurring such huge losses due to unethical conduct. The act put stricter rules in place for nominating board of director candidates and created a higher standard of accountability for corporate executives. Under the rules established in Sarbanes-Oxley, CEOs and CFOs must sign off on the financial statements to certify that the reports are a material representation of the corporation's financial position. With this change, CEOs and CFOs can no longer use the excuse that they are not accountants and do not understand the financial statements. It is now the duty of these executives to seek help if needed in understanding the financials in order to reassure stockholders that the information they are receiving is truthful.

NOTE: When General Motors was temporarily taken over by the government in 2009, the corporate officers failed the stockholders as the stockholders lost all of their investments. The moral dilemma faced by the government was whether the government had more of a duty to employees or the shareholders. The government sided with the 1.5 million employees.

Relationship with Employees

Since the Industrial Revolution, there has been a significant shift in corporate responsibility for employees and, in turn, expectations for employees. The key duties an employer has to its employees include providing a safe workplace, equal opportunities for jobs and advancement, protection against discrimination, and attention to quality-of-life matters.

Quality-of-life matters covers different areas, among which are time commitments and work-life balance. Any company that has 50 or more employees is required to offer up to 12 weeks of time off per year for the birth of a child, adoption, becoming a foster parent, or when caring for a seriously ill spouse or relative. This benefit was made possible as a result of the **Family and Medical Leave Act of 1993**. This leave can be paid or unpaid, depending upon the company's policy. Smaller employers try to help with a work-life balance by offering flexible hours, which includes flextime, compressed workweeks, job sharing, and telecommuting. Due to the COVID-19 pandemic, remote work and hybrid home/office work schedules are emerging quality-of-life benefits.

In trying to set the tone for ethical behavior, many companies have created **codes of conduct** that provide employees with an overall framework for expectations and acceptable behavior in the workplace. If signed by the employee, these codes become a legal agreement between the corporation and the employee. Such codes usually are not elaborate and work best when aligned with information in a company handbook.

Companies are legally bound to provide a minimum wage. A socially responsible company will pay what is known as a **living wage**—a wage that allows the employee to maintain a "normal" standard of living. However, even socially responsible corporations are not always able to pay that amount.

In return for this compensation, employees have a duty to demonstrate honesty, integrity, and loyalty to the company. This is a psychological contract where employees are implicitly expected to uphold these morals. It is expected that employees work the hours assigned or the hours necessary to complete the work without doing personal business during those hours. It is expected that employees be loyal to the company and the work. It is expected that employees demonstrate integrity by doing what they say they will do and accept responsibility when they don't.

NOTE: Ethical issues arise when an employee is so loyal that they overlook unethical behavior on the part of corporate leadership. If there is an opportunity, a motive, and a rationalization, the chances of unethical conduct occurring increases.

As part of the psychological contract, employees are entitled to fair and honest performance appraisals. Depending upon the way a company is structured and the work being performed, these performance appraisals can occur as annual reviews, promotional reviews, or on an as needed basis. As part of this review process, employers address factors that can affect employee happiness, such as reasonable compensation, job security, an ethical corporate culture, and clearly communicated expectations.

Dissatisfied employees are less productive and, thus, have a negative effect on the company's bottom line. General ways to reinforce a healthy corporate culture are keeping levels of competition among employees down, repeating communications, and providing an employee handbook. However, employee motivation is at times difficult to address.

One of the most common theories on how corporate leadership can best motivate employees is **Douglas McGregor's XY theory**. McGregor was an American social psychologist that theorized that managers fall into one of two ways of thinking about employees. The X managers believe that the average worker prefers to receive instructions, avoids responsibility, takes little initiative, and views money and job security as the only valid motivators. Y managers, on the other hand, view workers as independent thinkers who seek fulfillment through their efforts and work success. According to McGregor, this type of worker performs well and has high morale when they are able to develop work objectives and goals alongside the manager and is then given the freedom to achieve those goals.

McGregor's theory is a reminder that there are natural rules for managing people and different styles of management that can be implemented to motivate employees.

Corporations and Consumers

Consumers are protected by the **Consumer Bill of Rights**, which states that consumers have four basic rights: (1) the right to choose, (2) the right to safety, (3) the right to be informed, and (4) the right to be heard.

NOTE: President John F. Kennedy first mentioned the four consumer rights in 1962.

The **right to choose** is based on the concept that consumers should have the right to choose from an available range of goods or services set at competitive prices. An example of the corporations respecting this right are those that are producing generic drugs. By providing less expensive drugs, these companies are seeking to provide consumers with more purchasing freedom.

The **right to safety** refers to the legal and ethical obligation that companies have to consumers to produce goods or services that meet safety standards. In other words, consumers have the right to assume that the product or service they are purchasing is safe, is free from harmful chemicals, and will not be hazardous to health or life. The legal aspect of this right involves product liability that companies are held to by the courts. Even if the harm caused by a product was unintentional or unforeseen, companies are legally liable to those injured.

The **right to be informed** is a moral and legal obligation for businesses to ensure that consumers have access to information in order to make good choices. Consumers have the right to assume that companies are providing them with the necessary knowledge about a product, such as important safety information, warranties, and proper operating instructions.

Consumers' **right to be heard** deals with free speech to express an opinion about the product, service, or company. It is only through this voice that consumers can affect the change they want or need. A corporation that is acting morally will give attention to this information.

Consumers have no duty to corporations. Their only moral obligation is to be fair when they give voice to complaints. A corporation that fully assures these rights are being met beyond what is required by law builds trust with the consumer. By being service centric, even when simply selling a product, a company obtains consumer concerns and ideas about the latest customer needs while retaining customers.

Consumer trust is what leads to brand loyalty and a company's success. Such moral responsibility costs the company less in the long run. A business develops this type of trust by having a strong sense of integrity through established and enforced internal ethics principles and policies. Companies do need to be careful to not distort or manipulate these consumer rights so as to appear caring, honest, and trustworthy. An example of this type of behavior is seen in product warranties. Many companies provide a warranty that they know will expire well before the product should have any issues. The warranty is a guise to obtain information about the consumer rather than to provide financial protection for the consumer against defects. The moral question is heightened when the information obtained from warranty submissions is sold to outside marketing companies.

The Corporation within the Community and the Public Good

Corporations do not exist in a vacuum. As such, they affect the communities in which they operate. This effect can be economical, environmental, or both. The economic effect comes from the paying of taxes to support the community, the company using community vendors and contractors, and employees patronizing local restaurants or other community-based businesses. In return, the community supports companies by providing them with a source for employees and other services. When companies go bankrupt or relocate, the community can be financially harmed.

In addition to financially hurting a community, corporations have the potential to cause environmental harm to a community and its citizens. Such harmful events include dumping chemicals into the water system or improperly burying toxic waste. Whether the acts are intentional or unknown, a corporation that does not consider the community's well-being can negatively impact generations of community members.

Ethical corporations understand that they have a duty to protect the community to which they belong. These same corporations also understand that the relationship between corporations and their communities is a co-dependent type of social/psychological contract. As a result of this important coexistence, some states offer the designation of **public benefit corporation (PBC)**. A PBC designation means that a corporation is focusing on more than just profits. A PBC focuses on environmental, social, and governance (ESG) decisions that will generate decent returns for stockholders.

Another way in which corporations are trying to support their communities is through corporate philanthropy. **Corporate philanthropy** is when a company helps out not-for-profit organizations by sharing part of its sales revenues or by donating some of the company's products, equipment, or employees' time. A good example of corporate philanthropy is Yoplait's support for the Susan G. Komen Race for the Cure foundation.

SOCIAL RESPONSIBILITIES OF A BUSINESS

This section will review the social responsibilities of a business, which includes moral and ethical stances, individual responsibilities within a business, global responsibilities of a business, sustainable business growth, and environmental responsibility. Approximately 10 percent of the questions on the DSST exam cover this topic.

Moral and Ethical Stances

Corporate philanthropy is one form of social responsibility. **Social responsibility** refers to a company's acceptance of the role that ethics play in its business and its obligations to consider consumer and societal well-being in relation to the company's performance and profits. Corporations that demonstrate social responsibility take the moral stance ensconced in the theory of utilitarianism that moral actions are based on decisions bringing the greatest happiness to the greatest number of people.

A duty to shareholders and a duty to the community can create a moral dilemma for companies when it comes to social responsibility. Remember, a moral dilemma exists when an individual has a choice of at least two different actions, each of which fit within the individual's moral compass. For corporate officers, that moral dilemma can arise when a social responsibility, such as helping the community prosper, interferes with the officer's duty to provide a dividend for shareholders. Some examples of companies taking a moral stance on current issues and choosing social responsibility include restaurants that include a calorie count on its menu items and a university that becomes a completely smoke-free campus. In both cases, the chosen socially responsible action taken may lead to lost revenue. The restaurant may lose some customers who do not appreciate being reminded of calories, and the university may lose tuition as students who smoke choose to go to school elsewhere.

Individual Responsibilities Within a Business

Individual responsibilities within a business include everyone working in the business. The company's board of directors and executive officers set the direction and example for social responsibility. Managers who report to executives and the employees who report to the managers have an obligation to support the socially responsible stance of the organization. Through their integrity, these individuals make sure that all work is accomplished in a socially responsible manner. They ensure that products are properly manufactured, customers are fully informed, and the community is not harmed by careless disregard of the corporation's direction for societal well-being.

Even though shareholders and consumers are not responsible for a business's social responsibility, they do have influence. Shareholders demonstrate this influence by the withdrawal of investments when the corporation acts in a socially irresponsible manner. Shareholders who remain can exert influence by their vote for board members. Consumers can influence a corporation through their buying practices. Even brand loyalty is in jeopardy when a consumer either believes a company is not acting socially responsibly or does not believe in the social cause being set forth.

NOTE: Nike took an initial hit from shareholders when it used Colin Kaepernick in a commercial ad for "Just Do It" after Kaepernick kneeled during the National Anthem. The ad was controversial for its social and political message to consumers to "Just Do It" even if it means sacrificing the things you love the most. In Kaepernick's case, it was sacrificing his football career. Opposers boycotted the brand, but new consumers showed support, greatly increasing Nike's sales. This led to new shareholders investing in the company, sending Nike's market price even higher than its previous high.

Global Responsibilities of a Business

Because companies today are either international or have some sort of interaction with vendors from different countries, many see a move toward global social responsibilities. Thus, the need to practice societal well-being on a worldwide scale is rapidly coming into focus. For international companies, the three main global responsibilities include (1) a **moral duty for humanitarian rights**, (2) **protection and sustainability of the environment**, and (3) a **duty to provide a return on shareholders' investments**.

Humanitarian rights include a moral duty to all humans—domestic and foreign employees, domestic and foreign investors, and the global community. In connection with the environment, global responsibility includes both protecting the existing global natural resources from damage as well as sustaining resources for the future.

The major driver for a business to be globally responsible is **social pressure**. Consumers and shareholders are the groups most responsible for applying this pressure. Politicians typically have only a small amount of influence, as their concerns are usually limited in scope to their own communities. A global, socially responsible business understands the value of diversity. Instead of seeing the world as many different and diverse communities, a globally responsible company sees diversity as creating a better whole. Such businesses understand the value of tolerance and acceptance of what diversity creates. **Diversity management** is the process of developing a positive business environment that values differences and similarities in order to maximize all employees' potential and meet company goals, including global social responsibility.

As a result of global responsibility, a **global economy** has emerged that establishes corporate principles relating to social responsibilities. The main benefit of this global economy emergence is that the standards of living have been increasing in the countries where these companies operate.

Sustainable Business Growth and Responsibility

The existence of business social responsibility has companies realizing that they have multiple duties to their stakeholders. If these different duties are not fulfilled, neither the company nor the environment will be sustained. When companies consume large amounts of energy, dispose of waste by-products, and use up a community's natural resources, the environment is harmed. This raises an important question: how long can the environment take such treatment before becoming unsustainable? If the depletion of natural resources continues, growth cannot be sustained. Companies and communities struggle. Permanent environmental damage occurs.

On a more positive note, research has shown that companies that are socially responsible and ethical tend to do much better in the areas of company growth, profits, and employee well-being. Such results help make them even more sustainable. In 1994, John Elkington coined the term **triple bottom line**. Using **three Ps—people**, **planet**, and **profit**—to not only describe what the term means, but also the goal of sustainability. The three Ps are an integral part of the PBC designation.

Profitability is still a corporation's first responsibility of the three Ps. The reason for its primacy is that to not earn profits defrauds its investors and causes societal harm when employees are dismissed and a community loses a source of income. However, the other two Ps are important for a company's sustainability. Corporations that take sustainability seriously do so because they are aware that to not do so causes stakeholders to disengage from the company. While companies are not responsible for political climate, they can affect positive change through practicing ethical sustainability. Economic viability is made possible with socially responsible and environmentally friendly actions.

REGULATION OF BUSINESS

This section will focus on the regulation of businesses, specifically theories that impact governmental regulation, the existence of conflicts of interest and when to disclose, the role of politics and political contributions, and governmental control over business activities. Approximately nine percent of the questions on the DSST exam cover this topic.

Theoretical Issues

The **public interest theory of regulation** argues that government intervention in markets is needed as a response to market failures and imperfections so as to promote general well-being rather than the interests of a few influential stakeholders. The **business interest theory of regulation,** on the other hand, says that government should intervene to ensure fair competition.

Government regulations include laws on business ownership, competition, employment, and product safety. Some of these regulations stem from the type of government under which a company is operating. For example, in communist countries, regulations are based upon the government's limitation on employee's rights. In exchange for giving up these rights, employees are protected against unemployment under the law. Monopolies are another example of government regulation. The government determines whether a monopoly is fair and how to regulate it. Under the free enterprise system, government regulates fair competition as people under this type of system are allowed to own businesses, and competition is the foundation of economic success.

NOTE: Until 2017, the FCC enforced rules prohibiting monopolies in the area of news communication; no single company was allowed to own both a TV station and a newspaper in the same market area. These prohibitions were eliminated in 2017.

Business and Politics

Government regulation of business is based not only on real ethical issues, but also perceived ethical issues. The three most significant ethical challenges encountered in the workplace are (1) conflicts of interest, (2) accountability, and (3) honesty and integrity.

A **conflict of interest** is a situation where an individual is in a position to potentially derive personal benefit from actions or decisions made in that position. In other words, a person's impartiality can be called into question due to a conflict between self-interest and professional interest.

Conflicts of interest may exist at any level within an organization. For example, a conflict may exist because of whom an employee is related to, especially if that relative seeks a position or a contract with the corporation. Oftentimes, conflicts of interest will exist with board members and top executives when they have their personal money invested in other corporations. Keep in mind that the while a conflict of interest may exist, it does not necessarily mean that an individual with a conflict will choose to act unethically in pursuit of self-interest. The conflict here is the *potential* to make professional decisions based upon what will support personal investments. This means that if a conflict of interest is not disclosed (i.e., made known or public), the conflict can be *perceived* as having been the basis for a particular decision, especially if the decision does not work out.

A good example of this type of conflict is when an executive corporate officer has an investment in another company that is bidding for a contract with the officer's corporation. If the corporate officer recommends the company in which they have an interest in for the contract, does not disclose the relationship, and the contract ends up costing the corporation more, then when the conflict is discovered, the perception will be that the officer is at fault for the overrun.

The best way to avoid conflicts of interest is to have executive officers and top management sign a **conflict of interest agreement**. These agreements provide the organization with necessary need-to-know information to determine when a key individual should be left out of the decision-making process or why an officer or executive might need to be recused from a particular business dealing. While not all employees within an organization are asked to sign conflict of interest agreements, any employee with any type of conflict of interest should disclose that fact to management.

Another aspect of business dealings that gets scrutinized involves contributions to political candidates or parties. Some argue that such contributions are morally right as the business has a fiduciary duty to its shareholders. Since government regulates business, shareholders can be harmed by overly burdensome regulations. When a business is not allowed to engage in the politics of business regulation, it prevents the organization from having a voice. Citizens' voices come from the power of voting, whereas a business's voice comes from its contributions.

The counterargument to such contributions by corporations is that some businesses gain undue influence, which then leads to too much power. Such power can interfere with competition from companies with less influence and fewer resources to make contributions. Less competition can hurt the economy as monopolies can occur. Such a diversion of company resources can also stunt the long-term growth of the company making such contributions. In addition, employees with differing political views may become dissatisfied with the organization and negatively affect the company's output.

Governmental Control Over Business Activities

Governments regulate businesses in the core areas of advertising, labor, environmental impact, privacy, and health and safety. Government also regulates businesses to ensure fair competition and to ensure that the economic markets run effectively. Because businesses are motivated by profit, government steps in to protect investors, employees, and the general public. The laws enacted on business activities are known as **government compliance regulation** on business.

Government compliance regulation can sometimes have unintended consequences. One such unintended consequence results in slow wage growth, especially for unskilled workers. Since a company is responsible for the costs associated with compliance, wages may be lower so a company can recoup the compliance costs. The *Affordable Care Act* is one such example of government compliance regulation. One of the intentions of the act was to make companies pay for medical insurance for part-time workers who worked 30 or more hours a week. However, an unintended consequence was that employers cut hours so that they were not required to pay for insurance. Not only are these employees getting less pay, they also still have no company-paid insurance.

NOTE: Not all unintended consequences are negative. When the US government banned certain products in aerosol cans, companies were forced to find
innovative ways to pump out their products.

Some foreign governments choose to place fewer regulations on businesses.
Those governments are considered to be **laissez faire**, which is a French
term that means "to not be involved." In instances where governments
realize that compliance laws are creating deeper issues, the government
lifts regulations, or **deregulates**, the affected industry.

EMPLOYER-EMPLOYEE RELATIONS

Approximately 20 percent of the questions on the DSST exam will cover
employer-employee relations. This includes confidentiality, whistleblowing, discrimination, affirmative action, sexual harassment, and at-will
employment. Questions will also cover the duties of corporate officers,
which includes workplace safety.

Confidentiality and Whistleblowing

When it comes to confidentiality, there is a two-way street between employers and employees. Employers have a duty to employees to safeguard personal
information such as social security numbers, addresses, official disciplinary
documents, and salaries. In attending to this duty, there are several actions
employers can take to ensure this information stays confidential.

Employee personal information should be kept in a locked file or in a locked
office, if in paper format. For electronic confidential data, the employer
should make sure that there is appropriate security on the software and
networks. Since cybersecurity cannot protect against all data breaches,
companies are now required to disclose all data breaches to all those who
may have been affected by the breach. This requirement is a result of the
Data Protection Act.

Confidentiality policies and agreements are another protective measure
that a company can create to protect employee confidential information.
Such policies should include training regarding the importance of not
sharing information or data with anyone, including one's spouse. Employees, likewise, have an ethical obligation to keep company information, such
as data on employees and customers, confidential. However, employees do
not need to keep court findings confidential, because court findings are a

matter of public record, even if a nondisclosure agreement has been signed for or against the company. A **nondisclosure agreement**, also known as a **confidentiality agreement**, is a contract by which one or more parties agree not to disclose confidential information that they have shared with each other as a necessary part of doing business together. Nondisclosure agreements that are signed by both the employer and the employee are beneficial because they create a binding legal contract. Such contracts then provide the employer with legal leverage should the employee divulge confidential information. Many of these signed contracts include language to the effect that the agreement continues for a specified period after the employee leaves the company.

> **NOTE:** The Family Education Rights and Privacy Act (FERPA) provides legal protection for students' information. The Health Insurance Portability and Accountability Act (HIPAA) is legal protection for patient privacy and protection of data.

There is one major exception regarding an employee's obligation to keep company information and data confidential. That exception is if the employee is whistleblowing on a company. **Whistleblowing** is the term used when an employee discloses to company executives, to government representatives, or to the media the illegal or unethical practices that are being committed by the company. The Sarbanes-Oxley Act of 2002 came about due to scandals in the late 1990s and early 2000s, and it provides whistleblowers with greater protection against retaliation by the company being exposed.

Along with moral motivation, a whistleblower must also possess the virtue of courage. Just because a person is in the right by stepping forward to disclose unethical practices in a company does not mean that this person will keep their job, even with the enactment of law. Such individuals may find themselves embattled in costly court cases and attempts to smear their good names. Simply leaking information about a company's wrongdoing to a nongovernment source or anonymously telling the media may not constitute whistleblowing. Someone not willing to reveal their identity creates a question about the individual's intent for disclosing.

However, many companies have ethical hotlines in place where employees can anonymously submit such information. Companies have these hotlines to encourage those who are fearful to come forward. It is an avenue for companies to be kept aware of unethical issues as they arise and to act quickly to mitigate such behavior.

Discrimination and Affirmative Action

A specific type of unethical behavior that occurs in business is discrimination. **Discrimination** in the workplace is the negative treatment of a job candidate or an employee due to bias. Legally, such bias occurs on the basis of race, color, religion, sex (including pregnancy, sexual orientation, or gender identity), national origin, age, disability, and genetic information (including family medical history). Those belonging to any of these groups belong to what is now known as **protected classes**. Title VII of the Civil Rights Act of 1964 began a series of laws banning discrimination against those in protected classes. The following table details laws that are in place to protect from discrimination.

Laws Against Discrimination		
Law	**Basis for Protection**	**Other Provision of Law**
Equal Pay Act of 1963	Gender	Equal compensation for equal work, required skills
Civil Rights Act, Title VII of 1964 & as amended by Equal Opportunity Act of 1972	Race Color Religion Sex National origin	Banned discrimination in hiring, compensation, training, promotion, and firing
Age Discrimination in Employment Act of 1967 (ADEA)	Aged 40 or older	Banned discrimination in hiring, compensation, training, promotion, and firing
Rehabilitation Act of 1973	Disability	Prohibits the federal government from discriminating against qualified individuals with disabilities
Vietnam Era Veterans Readjustment Act of 1974	Disabled veterans	Affirmative action in employment and retention
Pregnancy Discrimination Act of 1978	Pregnant women and new mothers	Equality in company benefits and employment actions

Law	Basis for Protection	Other Provision of Law
Americans with Disabilities Act of 1990 (ADA)	Disability	Banned discrimination in employment, public accommodations, transportation, and telecommunications
Civil Rights Act of 1991 (CRA)	Expanded Civil Rights Act of 1964 to include punitive damages for sexual harassment	Put onus on employer to prove discrimination did not occur
Uniformed Services Employment & Reemployment Act of 1994	Employees' membership in or obligation to serve in uniformed services	Veterans, reservists, and National Guard members now able to reclaim job if absence due to service or training
Genetic Information Nondiscrimination Act of 2008	Genetic information	Includes nondiscrimination if genetic defect either in individual applicant/employee or applicant/employee's family
Lilly Ledbetter Fair Pay Act of 2009	Pay discrimination	Addressed when pay discrimination charges can be filed with Equal Employment Opportunity Commission (EEOC)

The **Civil Rights Act of 1991** was important because it put the burden of proof for nondiscrimination upon the employer. Neither the original Civil Rights Act nor the updated Civil Rights Act, while protecting on the basis of gender, specifically banned discrimination on the basis of sexual orientation. However, in June 2020, the US Supreme Court issued a landmark decision in *Bostock v. Clayton County* that the prohibition against sex discrimination in Title VII of the Civil Rights Act includes employment discrimination against an individual on the basis of sexual orientation or transgender status.

Other forms of discrimination that still are allowed in the workplace include discrimination on the basis of political affiliation, height, and weight. While dress codes overall are becoming passé, it is not illegal to have a dress code as long as it is not discriminatory in nature.

Before the **Age Discrimination Act**, some businesses discriminated against older workers because employers found it less expensive to hire younger workers. Older workers earn higher wages, while their health care insurance and other benefits cost more than that of younger workers. Some companies are now utilizing a loophole in the Age Discrimination Act, offering incentives for early retirement to older workers only, reassigning older workers to departments in which they don't wish to work, and unfairly rating older workers more harshly than younger workers on performance evaluations. It is difficult to prove that the basis for these actions is due to a bias against older workers. In fairness to other companies, they are being ethical when they see a gap in the older worker's technology skills, for example. These companies require—but also pay for—the retraining of older workers.

In the 1960s, President Lyndon B. Johnson signed executive orders promoting affirmative action. **Affirmative action** is a plan to ensure businesses provide employment opportunities for those from groups that have historically faced discrimination. An example of an affirmative action plan is where statistical analysis is used to make sure a company creates a workforce that reflects the demographics of the organization's service area. By ensuring the labor pool is a reflection of the service area, there is a better chance of hiring individuals from protected classes. This is why affirmative action is also called **positive discrimination**.

There is often the misconception that affirmative action requires employers to hire individuals from protected classes whether the candidate is qualified or not. While the applicant does not have to be the most qualified candidate, affirmative action does require that the applicant be qualified for the position. An unintended result of affirmative action is *reverse discrimination*. The argument that reverse discrimination exists is that affirmative action places the focus on racial, gender, age, and veteran-related issues instead of finding the best fit for the position.

Sexual Harassment

Sexism occurs when individuals are treated differently based on gender. Sexism can become discrimination when it occurs in the workplace. Sex discrimination and sexual harassment are often confused as synonyms for one another. While sexual harassment is a type of sex discrimination, **sex discrimination** involves work-related decisions based on gender. **Sexual harassment**, on the other hand, refers to work-related decisions that specifically are based on unwelcome sexual advances or inappropriate sexual remarks. It wasn't until 1986 that the Supreme Court equated sexual harassment with sex discrimination. Before 1986, sexual harassment was not illegal.

In legal terms, sexual harassment includes unwelcome and inappropriate actions of a sexual nature in the workplace. There are two distinct types of action involved in harassment. The first are unwelcome physical advances that may include *quid pro quo*, which is a Latin term meaning "something for something." **Quid pro quo sexual harassment** involves someone within a company who is higher up in the organization or has supervisory duties who pressures an employee to comply with unwelcome physical advances in return for job security. In this case, the *quid pro quo* for sexual favors is maintaining employment or obtaining advancement.

The second aspect of sexual harassment includes inappropriate actions such as displaying materials of a sexual nature in the workplace that others find offensive. These actions can also be verbal or nonverbal and create a hostile work environment. A **hostile work environment** is created when an employee is expected to endure pervasive, offensive, discriminatory conduct of any kind that becomes a condition of employment and that a reasonable person would find intimidating. A hostile work environment based on gender is clearly a type of sexual harassment. Both men and women can be victims of sexual harassment.

NOTE: For the fiscal year 2021, approximately 16% of the yearly sexual harassment complaints received by the EEOC are filed by males. See www.eeoc.gov/statistics/charges-alleging-sex-based-harassment-charges-filed-eeoc-fy-2010-fy-2021.

There are actions that an employer can take to avoid liability for a hostile work environment. The employer must take reasonable care to prevent the harassment in the first place, must take prompt corrective action to stop the harassment, and must prove that the wrongdoing employee unreasonably refused to take advantage of corrective action.

A company is morally obligated to ban sexual harassment in the workplace because a company is seen as an entity unto itself. As such, the moral expectation is that a company will treat employees the way in which the company wishes to be treated—the golden rule at work. It is for this reason that an employer has a duty to intervene in any situation in which an employee is being sexually harassed, whether by a manager, a coworker, a vendor, or a customer.

If a supervisor or manager receives a report of sexual harassment, they should immediately report the information to the human resources department. If a manager does not do so, the company becomes legally liable for the harassment. Companies should also have a sexual harassment policy. Such a policy should contain a definition of sexual harassment that describes types of verbal, nonverbal, and physical sexual harassment; the company's stance on consensual relations within the organization; the complaint procedure; and a statement of alternative remedies in addition to legal remedies.

NOTE: The Civil Rights Act dealing with discrimination (that now includes sexual harassment as a form of discrimination) applies to employers with 15 or more employees. However, state laws tend to cover all other small businesses.

Duties of Corporate Officers

A corporate officer has moral obligations to exercise due diligence in actions on behalf of the corporation and reasonable prudence in carrying out their duties to achieve the best interests of the corporation, in addition to fiduciary duties to shareholders. These moral obligations are not only to shareholders but also to employees.

The biggest obligation is the overall **health and safety** of the employees. Remember, the corporate officer is responsible for the overall operations and resources of the business and not the minute details of looking at every piece of equipment to ensure it is operating safely. Instead, the corporate officer is meeting their moral obligation for employee safety by ensuring the workplace has **health and safety guidelines** in place that are enforced.

For example, a university president is fulfilling their duty if there is a policy in place for whenever a deadly contagious disease is disclosed. The policy might include a thorough disinfecting of classrooms, along with notification to faculty and staff. If such a situation arises and the president discovers that either the rooms were not disinfected or no notification was sent, they would be acting responsibly by dismissing those who failed to follow the policy.

In addition to guidelines, the corporate officer should ensure that a **safety plan** includes regular training, the resources necessary to carry out the training, and communications about safety. Today's corporate officer is bound by stricter regulations than in the past. Many of these health and safety regulations come from the **Occupational Safety and Health Administration (OSHA)**. OSHA was created to develop and enforce safety and health regulations for businesses in the United States. OSHA requires that training takes place, and that employers ensure their employees understand health and safety procedures and why these procedures are in place.

OSHA requires detailed record-keeping of injuries and fatalities that occur in the workplace. If the cases are not dealt with appropriately, or if the number of injuries does not fit within acceptable guidelines, OSHA can fine the employer. For this reason, employers will reprimand employees for safety violations or give bonuses if the company is accident free for a specified period.

Another aspect of workplace safety involves keeping the workplace free of violence. While much is heard about former employees coming back to the business to commit violence against management or coworkers, workplace violence has also been perpetrated by relatives of an employee, dissatisfied customers, vendors who were not given a chance to be a supplier, and even disgruntled shareholders. Again, corporate officers can develop appropriate policies that cover all these various groups. For example, the policy might include the requirement that anyone except current employees must sign in at a front desk and be screened as to their reason for being in the building.

Labor Relations

Labor relations between employers and employees can be contentious at times. Historically, when the Industrial Revolution shifted business from farm to factories, little was known about formal management and leadership. The bottom line for big business was to generate a profit. For the average worker, getting steady pay seemed great. However, employer ignorance with regard to motivation, a lack of understanding regarding moral duties, and some outright abuses of workers in an effort to gain profit led these workers to begin questioning working conditions. As a result, unions were formed.

A **union** is a group of workers, not necessarily from the same company, who band together to achieve common goals in the areas of wages, hours, and working conditions, such as the use of child labor. A **union contract** is a formal agreement between a company's management and its employees that serves as a guide to their relationship, with the rights of each party clearly spelled out. Before companies truly started working with unions, the government stepped in with the **National Labor Relations Act of 1935 (NLRA)**, also known as the **Wagner Act**, that legalized collective bargaining. **Collective bargaining** is the negotiation process between company management and union representatives. Section I of the National Labor Relations Act describes unfair labor practices that can come from the employer or from union representatives.

Other laws followed the NLRA to ensure both employers and unions were working together in the interest of the worker and not the particular institution, as unethical practices arose among unions.

Important Government Regulations on Labor

Name of the Law	Effects on Employers/Employees/Unions	Other Important Facts
National Labor Relations Act of 1935	• Prevents employee dismissal for joining union • Prohibits employers from interfering in unionization • Bans employers from refusing to bargain	Established the National Labor Relations Board (NLRB) to supervise union elections
Fair Labor Standards Act of 1938	• Prohibits employers from hiring child labor • Set a minimum wage for employees at 25 cents per hour	Established a maximum workweek for particular industries
Labor Management Relations Act of 1947 (an amendment to the 1935 Wagner Act)	• Prohibits unions from coercing workers to join • Bans unions from trying to force employers to discriminate against nonunion workers • Prevents unions from charging excessive initiation fees • Bans unions from striking or picketing for noncontractual, illegal purposes	Also called the Taft-Hartley Act of 1947
Labor-Management Reporting and Disclosure Act of 1959 (LMRDA)	• Requires unions to have a constitution and hold regular meetings • Requires unions to have secret ballots when voting for union officials	Also known as the Landrum-Griffin Act of 1959 Provides a bill of rights for union members

NOTE: According to the National Labor Relations Board, union officials face a disproportionally high number of allegations of wrongdoing when compared to employers. The vast majority of allegations were from members who were hurt by the very union that was supposed to protect them.

Even with these regulations in place, there are practices on the part of both management and the unions where each tries to get its way. For the union, there are pickets and strikes. For management, there are lockouts. Ethical dilemmas are often the result. For example, if a company decides to lock out its unionized employees over a union labor dispute, the company must also consider whether to allow the company to possibly go out of business, with consequences for the company owners, other employees, and the surrounding community.

Because most union contracts include bylaws that employees can only be dismissed for just cause, the question arose as to how long an employer must keep an employee. As a result, states began enacting **at-will employment**. Such laws allow an employer to dismiss an employee at any time for any (or for no reason), if the reason is not discriminatory in nature, and there is no written employment agreement that provides conditions under which an employee can be let go. Likewise, an employee has the right to leave an employer at any time for any reason (or no reason) if they do not have a signed agreement and the company is located in an at-will state.

Even in at-will states, protections are put in place to protect workers and the community when a large layoff is about to occur. The **Worker Adjustment and Retraining Notification Act of 1988 (WARN)** requires most companies with 100 or more employees to notify those employees and the community 60 calendar days in advance of a closing or massive layoff. This law gives the community time to develop plans to counter any negative effects to the community's economy and provide workers with resources on finding new positions.

ETHICS OF INFORMATION

This section will explore the ethics of information related to the areas of marketing, advertising, corporate espionage, cybersecurity, privacy, proprietary information, and information technology. Approximately 16 percent of the questions on the DSST exam cover this topic.

Marketing and Advertising

As noted earlier, one of the four rights that consumers have is the right to be informed. As such, a business has a moral obligation to ensure that it is communicating in an honest manner with consumers. A business communicates with consumers through marketing and advertising. Just as the ethics towards employees has evolved over time, so too has the ethics of marketing and advertising.

Prior to the 1940s, businesses relied on product advertising. The belief was that the product would sell itself. Due to this belief, marketing did little to inform consumers about the product other than to advertise the product's existence. Ethical businesses concentrated on the idea of ensuring a product lasted, and the product itself was safe. Between the early 1940s and through the 1980s, the sales era evolved to promote the premise that selling would overcome any consumer resistance. Marketing communication increased, but often issues would arise as to the truthfulness behind the selling tactics.

In the 1990s, the relationship era of marketing came into being. Marketing became rooted in the idea that long-term relationships with consumers would lead to success. Service became a large aspect of value added to the product. Marketing further increased its communications toward consumers with information on how the product worked, average life span of the product, and how to keep the product working. Advertising evolved to include celebrity endorsement of products, with the ethical issue centered on truth in advertising. Today's marketing era is known as the social era, as the emphasis is on connecting with consumers through social media.

Businesses now have a moral obligation to not only ensure truth in advertising but also to ensure that their message is being delivered to the correct consumer groups. For example, online businesses must ensure that products marked for age 18 and over are advertised to the appropriate age group *and* are not getting into the hands of minors. Marketing departments must selectively market, i.e., target their advertising to certain select groups. This is known as **selective marketing**. Selective marketing raises the ethical question as to who may be excluded from product knowledge.

Another part of marketing is **pricing strategy**. A practice known as **skimming** allows companies to recuperate some of their research costs, especially when a product is new, there is little competition, and consumers are willing to pay a higher price for the product. Ethical challenges can occur when skimming is paired with advertising that is not truthful. For example, a manufacturer may produce and charge an exorbitant amount for a product with a defect unknown to the public. The company is able to charge a higher price because consumers want the product and there is little or no competition to interfere. Pharmaceutical companies have recently come under fire for a type of medical skimming, where they raise prices on commonly needed drugs in order to cover the associated costs for researching new drugs.

There are many different types of unethical advertising practices. As the government puts regulations in place, unethical businesses find loopholes or other ways not to be truthful. An example of such a practice is the use of shills. A **shill** is someone, often a celebrity or a social media influencer, who makes a sales pitch or serves as a promoter of a product. Where ethics come into play is when the shill includes a false endorsement or review for a product. Government regulations are now in place that ban celebrities from saying or implying that they have used a product when they in real life have not. Such celebrity endorsements are difficult to prove and therefore rarely brought before a court.

Research has shown that, while unethical marketing and advertising can bring about excellent short-term profits, the long-term effect on profit is negative. For example, few diet pills can achieve the type of results that consumers seek. Thus, misleading statements that prey on what the consumer is seeking (e.g., large weight loss in no time) will quickly bring in business and profit. However, the profit will be short-lived as consumers realize that the product does not live up to expectations. Ethical advertising, on the other hand, leads to long-term, steady profit.

Corporate Espionage and Cybersecurity

Corporate espionage, also called **industrial espionage**, **economic espionage**, or **corporate spying**, is the term used when a company uses spying techniques on other companies to obtain confidential information for commercial or financial gain. An example of corporate espionage is a company sending one of its employees to a competitor to pose as a potential client or employee. This type of action is unethical because it invades a company's right to privacy of confidential information, and it can create an unfair competitive advantage because the target company has already spent the effort and money to develop or improve a product or process. This type of action also violates the morality of justness. Justness involves acting fairly.

Spying techniques can include trespassing onto a competitor's property without their knowledge or permission, the disclosure of trade secrets from an insider to a competitor, wiretapping, hacking into a computer or network, or attacking a competitor's website with **malware**, which is software that is specifically designed to disrupt, damage, or gain unauthorized access. **Spyware** gathers information through internet connections without the user being aware. With spyware, companies are able to secretly obtain information on other companies' employees, customers and vendors, and other businesses involved with that particular company. Some spyware is used to covertly gather information about an organization. The information is then sold to other companies.

Not all spyware use is unethical. For example, spyware that allows a company to filter access to particular sites on company computers is morally and legally acceptable, as long as the company informs its employees. Spyware that is used for marketing purposes has come under question as to its morality. In such cases, the spyware uses tracking pixels that secretly allows it to see whether one has opened an email from the company, how long it took for the email to be read, and how often an individual returns to read the email.

If a company wants to ethically uncover information about a client, it can use what is called **intelligent fact-finding**. Such fact-finding can be obtained by analyzing public records and surveying a competitor's clients, as long as the company clearly identifies itself and its purpose. Such company "spying" is especially popular in some countries. Regulatory provisions, for example, could be used to extract information through backdoor encryption technology. Some foreign countries, such as China, require foreign businesses to turn over their source code and encryption software, exploiting a legally mandated backdoor. According to the 2017 Commission on the Theft of Intellectual Property, China has been the biggest offender for cyber theft of corporate secrets and information.

The implementation of cybersecurity measures helps to prevent losses associated with unethical conduct associated with the unauthorized access or use of electronic data. **Cybersecurity** is the state of being protected against the criminal or unauthorized use of electronic data. Cybersecurity is important because it protects all categories of data from theft and damage. This includes sensitive data, personally identifiable information, protected health information, personal information, intellectual property, and information systems. It is typically classified into five distinct types of protection: (1) critical infrastructure security, (2) application security, (3) network security, (4) cloud security, and (5) internet of things (IoT) security. Businesses have an ethical duty to implement a cybersecurity model that protects confidentiality, integrity, and availability.

Privacy Issues and Concerns

In the age of digital media and technology, the issue of the right to privacy and how to protect that right is constantly in play. Both employees and consumers have a certain expectation that their personal information will be kept private. Unfortunately, data breaches are a common occurrence.

The **General Data Protection Regulation** was enacted to provide a comprehensive data regulation on international companies. This regulation was created by the European Union in 2018 and affects any organization wanting to do business in Europe. The regulation controls data protection along with privacy. One requirement of this law is that businesses must have a cybersecurity system in place if they want to have business dealings in the European Union countries.

The **US Privacy Act** does not regulate data to the extent that the General Data Protection Regulation does. Under the US Privacy Act, businesses can gather information on any person and combine it for a profile, as long as the person has clicked on a terms' agreement button. By agreeing to the terms, individuals give up their right to certain privacies.

However, websites and apps collecting personal information to sell to different businesses for marketing purposes brings up an interesting ethical privacy question. While most sites do request that individuals click to accept the terms for the use of the site, the ethical issue here is whether *buried* terms of agreement are sufficient, especially when it comes to privacy. Consumers concerned with privacy issues are best served when they carefully read these terms for usage and make decisions based upon how their information might be used. But how many consumers actually read the terms of agreement, and furthermore, understand the terms they are agreeing to?

While the rights theory states that individuals are entitled to the right of privacy, and that right is extended to the workplace, employees cannot expect total privacy on the job. Instead, employees have the right to *reasonable privacy*. In the US, employees can expect reasonable privacy from video and recordings of personal interactions. US law also requires businesses to inform employees of any surveillance and recording, and the purpose of the recording. This purpose statement is key to ensuring an employee's privacy. For example, if an employer suspects an employee of wrongdoing, the employer cannot begin recording the employee's phone calls without notification and the reason for doing so. In the process of recording phone calls for quality assurance, an employer is not allowed to record personal calls that the employee may make. Even if something is caught accidently while recording for quality assurance, the employer cannot use the guise of quality assurance to capture personal activities.

This right to personal privacy extends to an employee's desk and locker. An employer cannot do a search without prior consent. Also, employers cannot do a background check unless the employer has obtained prior consent from the employee. A good example of a situation that may feel as though personal privacy is being violated is the requirement that purses or bags must either be in clear plastic or go through a security check. However, in such cases, employees know ahead of time about the search and the need to see what is brought in or out of the business for security reasons or to protect intellectual property. Both notification and purpose are present in this example.

Control of Proprietary Information

Proprietary information is any information that a company wishes to keep confidential. Proprietary information includes employee and customer personal information and data that a company has a moral obligation to keep private. It also includes trade secrets that a company may have, such as formulas, processes, intellectual property, customer lists, or any type of data or information that a company wants to keep private for whatever reason. Once information is public, such as government contracts or patents on products or processes, the information is no longer considered proprietary since it is now freely available.

The **Economic Espionage Act of 1996** defined trade secrets as including written material on processes that the owner has taken reasonable effort to keep from the public and that has economic value. This act was intentionally written to protect proprietary information. If this act is violated, there are stiff financial fines as well as possible imprisonment.

The biggest threats to keeping proprietary information on computer networks secret include e-crime and malware. **E-crime** includes an individual or company hacking into another company's networks to either obtain proprietary information or to maliciously have the information disappear. **Malware** includes any type of software that is intended for unethical purposes. Specific types of malware include Trojan horses, viruses, worms, botnets, and other types of spyware.

There are several tools available for companies to protect information from these types of threats. The Chief Information Officer (CIO) is the executive officer responsible for creating a comprehensive plan for proprietary information protection. To create such a plan, the CIO or individual identified as being responsible must first identify all the information of the company that is proprietary. To build good controls, the plan should allow access to the information only to those employees and outside people who have a need to know. The plan also needs to include the requirement that those employees and vendors or outside parties sign nondisclosure agreements.

A signed **nondisclosure agreement** legally binds employees and vendors from discussing proprietary information and ensures safeguards are in place so that such information is not overheard or breached. If a company's data is breached, the CIO should also have a fully developed disaster recovery plan. Such preplanning can help the company navigate quickly through necessary notifications, especially if the proprietary information includes employee or customer data and backup plans on how to recover the data. The disaster recovery plan should also include information on legal actions and back-up plans on how to recover the competitive edge that the proprietary information afforded them.

Information Technology Regulations

The lack of consistent and widespread regulation of the internet and computer technology, particularly in the areas of data privacy and security, has reached a crisis point. In 2018, the issue of regulating the internet by limiting harmful content, addressing privacy concerns, safeguarding the integrity of elections, and ensuring data portability came to a head when Facebook CEO Mark Zuckerberg was called to testify before Congress regarding the unauthorized collection and use of Facebook user data. Cambridge Consulting, a British consulting firm, had used data they collected without consent from either Facebook or an estimated 87 million Facebook users to influence elections. Zuckerberg also admitted that the Facebook platform had been used by the Russians to spread propaganda and fake news.

This high-profile case highlighted the need for revised guidelines to govern the regulation of technologies and their products and services. The current federal framework is outdated by more than 20 years. The last major legislation to address the activities of the communications and IT industries was the **Telecommunications Act of 1996**. While this act deregulated the communications industry, it did not address data privacy other than to prohibit local exchange service from recording calls or using the contents of calls for the purposes of marketing. The internet and social media were in their infancy in the late 90s.

The US government has attempted to regulate and address cybersecurity issues through the enactment of the **Cybersecurity Information Sharing Act (CISA)**, the **Cybersecurity Enhancement Act of 2014**, the **Federal Exchange Data Breach Notification Act of 2015**, and the **National Cybersecurity Protection Advancement Act of 2015**. However, none of the legislation addresses computer-related industries, internet-service providers, or software companies, including those companies that create and run social media sites. Subsequently, ethical issues and misconduct abound regarding the use, tracking, and handling of consumer data. Consumers have the right to be protected from unfair business practices. It is a corporation's duty to ensure that the rights of consumers are protected, and they are informed of any ethical breaches.

BUSINESS ETHICS IN A GLOBAL ECONOMY

This section will briefly explore business ethics in a global economy. This includes a review of corporate citizenship, ethics in national corporations, outsourcing and offshoring, ethical standard in different countries, and fair trade laws and standards. Approximately 16 percent of the questions on the DSST exam cover this topic.

Corporate Citizenship

Hobbes' social contract theory, as mentioned earlier, basically explains that every citizen within a society tacitly agrees to give up a right to everything in nature in order to live in an orderly society. Thus, moral behavior is based on following the norms of one's society. However, what happens when that society is larger than a community, state, or country? According to **Immanuel Kant's Moral Theory**, consequences do not determine whether an action is moral or not, but rather if the action meets or fulfills an individual's duty. Kant's theory helps explain why and how companies become more than an international or global company but move to become global citizens.

Global corporate citizenship refers to a corporation's legal and political responsibilities for operating in a global economy. A global corporate citizen is a corporation acting as a long-term stakeholder in a global society. These corporate citizens promote the removal of trade barriers so that global consumers have the best opportunity to improve their standard of living. Global corporate citizens desire the improvement of economic conditions for all countries.

The United Nations **Global Compact** is a corporate citizen network set up to promote worldwide corporate responsibility. Like other corporate citizens, those belonging to the Global Compact will try to ensure business profits while also trying to do no harm. Global corporate citizens follow global ethics. **Global ethics** is defined as the values and norms that concern world poverty, environmental problems, peace and security, and human rights.

Global corporate citizens, then, concentrate their efforts on people and their well-being, environmental issues, and discrimination. While much attention has been given to child labor issues, age and sex discrimination have not been much of a focus of global social responsibility. According to research, safety has had the least effort from global citizens. **Greenwashing** has become an ethical challenge in the global arena. Greenwashing is the term used when a company uses advertising and reputation marketing to make it appear to be a socially responsible global citizen (specifically for environmental practices) when in reality it is not.

Ethics in Transnational Corporations

Global corporate citizens can be found in both international and transnational corporations. Corporate citizenship may be stronger in **transnational corporations** as such companies have no identifiable home country base, whereas **international corporations** still have a strong national identification. Transnational corporations are interested in most markets; they do not focus only on the market in a specific country. As such, they are not controlled by nationals of any specific country.

As a result, a unique ethical issue arises when attempting to determine which country's culture to use as a basis for behavior. The **Foreign Corrupt Practices Act of 1977** bans the bribery of officials in order to set up a branch of a business in another country. One legal way in which transnational corporations have gotten around this ban is to license a company in a new market to produce and sell its product. The transnational corporation earns revenue from the licensing and royalty fees. It is then up to the new company to pay off its government officials according to that home-based country's norms. The transnational corporation has now avoided identifying with a particular country's norms and values through this backdoor method.

So how can a transnational corporation help developing countries and be a global citizen? In the case of licensing, the transnational business can help get the economy going in a developing country. By expanding business in this manner, it provides work for that country's citizens. In order to get the company up and running, the transnational corporation also has to develop roads and improve other infrastructures to ensure the parts for the product can be delivered and the goods produced can be shipped. Such infrastructure greatly improves the living standards of a developing country. One ethical consideration that a transnational corporation needs to face to be socially responsible is the impact on workers. Companies need to consider whether their actions will benefit or harm the workers in developing countries. While a new business can bring work opportunities for unskilled workers, unskilled workers can also be forced into work that they do not desire to perform and be forced to work under what is essentially slave conditions.

Outsourcing and Offshoring

Domestic companies will often outsource or offshore some aspect of their business before becoming international companies. While the two terms are often used interchangeably, there is a difference. **Outsourcing** involves using vendors for goods or services previously handled in-house or in-country. These vendors may be in the same country as the company, or they may be in a foreign country. **Offshoring**, on the other hand, is about the relocation of business processes outside of the country in which the company resides. Offshoring, then, is one possible means of outsourcing.

Companies that outsource through offshoring face the same ethical issues that transnational corporations need to consider. Outsourcing can be beneficial for both the business that outsources and the business to which the work is outsourced. However, by not investigating the working conditions of the company to which the work is outsourced, the possibility of child labor, lack of safety, or discrimination must be considered. Sweat shops are the major ethical concern when it comes to outsourcing to foreign countries.

Another ethical issue that can arise in offshoring centers on the consumer. A company needs to consider whether the quality of service will suffer before offshoring. Remember, consumers have the right to be informed. If language barriers interfere with that right, a corporation's duty to its customers will not be fulfilled, and profits will most likely decline as consumers seek another company from which to purchase products.

The benefit of offshoring is globalization, which in effect raises standards of living. The company that outsources can save labor costs, while workers in developing countries can earn a living wage. The result is an improvement in economic conditions for the country. However, while the Foreign Corrupt Practices Act bans many activities, it does not ban the lobbying of politicians in both the home country and the outsourced country in order to try to initiate or influence legislation.

Ethical Standards in Different Countries

As described by Hobbes' social contract theory, every society has different norms and values. As such, operating internationally means running into different standards and finding ways to either manage those differences or to not do business within certain countries. Therefore, minimum social, economic, and environmental requirements have been set as fair trade standards in the global economy. Minimum governmental requirements are not included in these requirements because of societal differences. It would be virtually impossible and morally wrong to require governments to have the exact same requirements just to have a global economy.

The most important ethical issues regarding these different standards center on human rights, employment practices, and corruption. **Human rights**, especially in developing countries, involve consideration of treatment of people and the basic rights afforded all humans: work hours, wages, and safety issues. Workers in many foreign countries are forced to work long hours with no breaks and under intolerable conditions with respect to temperature and safety. These individuals earn little to no wages in exchange for a small area in which to sleep. This is considered **slave labor**.

Human rights and employment practice differences are the two most ethically significant issues that cause concern among global corporate citizens. While there are ethical differences in what is considered corruption in different countries, it is not as concerning as the health and well-being of people. In addition, in countries such as in the US where corruption is viewed as morally wrong by its social contract, there are regulations such as the Foreign Corrupt Practices Act that provide a solution to this type of difference in ethical standards, making it illegal.

The best way to counter these ethical differences is for a company to operate internationally based upon the practices and values of its home country. An international company can avoid violating its own values through corporate governance that includes developing, implementing, and enforcing codes of conduct.

Fair Trade Laws and Standards

In order to assist developing countries and build international goodwill, businesses will often establish themselves in foreign nations. This helps to open up markets in highly-developed nations, allowing consumers the chance to obtain lower-priced goods. These imports create fair competition, which then leads to innovation.

Both within and between countries, fair trade requires ethical actions. In the US, fair trade laws first started in the states. California was the first state to create a statute that regulated trade between manufacturers and retailers coming in from other states in order to ensure producers could make a decent livelihood. These state fair trade laws set a minimum retail price on products.

The various state fair trade laws eventually led to the **Miller-Tydings Act of 1937**, which exempts fair trade from antitrust laws. As companies became more international, the fair trade movement became a means to help developing countries. Fair trade provides a market for goods produced by refugees and other disadvantaged groups, to help improve the quality of life of these workers. Governments in developed countries began subsidizing imports from less developed countries. Some countries, though, began dumping their products into these new markets at extremely low prices. This prompted changes to the fair trade practices, allowing governments of the countries to counter by increasing import duties to offset subsidies.

Even though trade barriers such as tariffs, quotas, and embargoes still exist, movement has been toward a free trade world. Various organizations and trade agreements between countries are gradually removing existing barriers. The moral argument for trade agreements is the mutual benefit of the countries involved. Even developed countries benefit from no tariffs and the increased need for skilled workers in the areas of logistics, supply-chain management, transportation, and retailing.

A multinational organization of industrialized countries formed in 1947 to help reduce trade barriers while improving protection for patents and copyrights. This organization is the **General Agreement on Tariffs and Trade (GATT)**. From this organization, the **World Trade Organization (WTO)** was created to monitor the agreements that came from GATT and to mediate international trade disputes. The four major areas of activity for the WTO include:

1. Trade negotiations
2. Monitoring multilateral trade agreements
3. Dispute settlement
4. Support for and development of trade capacity

The WTO is not a government body, and it does not create or develop trade agreements.

NOTE: In 2001, China was allowed to enter the WTO even though it had a poor record on human rights. Twenty years later, China's membership is controversial and contentious due to numerous allegations of repeated violations to its agreement with WTO.

The WTO is not in the business of financing the breaking down of trade barriers. The **World Bank** was created to help encourage fair trade through financing, especially for developing countries. It was established by industrialized nations to lend money to less developed countries to build or expand infrastructures such as transportation, education, and medical systems. It is difficult for a developing country to make and sell products if there is no system in place to help educate the people, and no means to get products to market.

Governmental bodies from different countries will enter into trade agreements. These agreements help break down tariffs and trade restrictions, especially between countries that share borders. One such example of a multilateral trade agreement was the **North American Free Trade Agreement (NAFTA)**. However, this agreement was controversial because while it improved the US economy in the areas of trade growth and investment, it hurt the economy in the areas of employment and balance of trade. In 2018, President Trump announced a new trade deal with Mexico to replace NAFTA that would maintain duty-free access for agricultural goods and eliminate nontariff barriers. The agreement was modified to include Canada in the later part of 2018 and the **United States-Mexico-Canada Agreement (USMCA)** replaced NAFTA on July 1, 2020. The USMCA expands the tariff ban on new technologies and industries. The agreement prohibits tariffs on digital music, ebooks, and other digital products, and also establishes copyright safe harbor for internet companies, meaning they can't be held liable for copyright infringements by users.

SUMMING IT UP

- **Business ethics**, also called **business morals**, is the standards of conduct and values governing decision-making and actions in the business environment.
- Three basic economic systems evolved as a result of differing opinions as to who should own and operate businesses: (1) the **free enterprise system** (privately owned), (2) **communism** (government owned), and (3) **socialism** (mostly government owned).
- The most common type of unethical behavior in corporations is related to financial statement misrepresentation.
    - o **Improper revenue recognition** includes improper timing of revenue recognition, fictitious revenues, inflated income due to one-time gains, nonrecognition of liabilities, improper recognition of expenses, and improper cash flow presentation. This type of fraud is usually committed by senior management or officers that have access to high-level financial information.
    - o **Misappropriation of assets** is the theft of an entity's assets for personal gain. This happens when trusted people within an organization abuse their authority and power to steal company or client assets through fraudulent activities.
- **Insider trading** involves individuals who have *inside* information that provides them with knowledge ahead of time of business dealings that might impact the value of company stock.
- Psychologist **Lawrence Kohlberg** identified that individuals typically develop moral standards in six different stages that can be grouped into three different levels of development. These stages are not dependent upon the ethical background a person has experienced.
    - o Stage 1: Obedience and Punishment (pre-conventional)
    - o Stage 2: Individualism and Exchange (pre-conventional)
    - o Stage 3: Good Interpersonal Relationships (conventional)
    - o Stage 4: Maintaining Social Order (conventional)
    - o Stage 5: Social Contract and Individual Rights (post-conventional)
    - o Stage 6: Universal Principles (post-conventional)
- An ethical corporation requires ethical leadership in accordance with **social and psychological contract theories**.
    - o A **social contract** is a framework for how individuals should behave in accordance with laws and certain expectations.
    - o A **psychological contract** is often implicit; it's a dynamic arrangement where individuals agree to give up certain behaviors and rights in agreement to follow a company's rules and processes.

- The three broad categories of ethical theory are **rights, consequentiality**, and **deontology.**
    - o Rights includes **relativism,** which is based on the idea that societal norms determine what is morally right.
    - o **Consequentiality** is based upon the idea that to be moral, a decision needs to be based upon the consequences of the chosen action.
    - o **Deontology** stems from **Immanuel Kant's theory** that morality does not stem from consideration of consequences. Morality is based on duty. Everyone has duties to others, and it is that duty that determines whether an action is right or wrong depending on whether that duty was fulfilled.
- Stakeholders include shareholders, employees, customers, vendors, and the community at-large. A corporation has a **fiduciary duty** to align the goals of its corporate officers with the shareholders, provide various protections for employees and customers, and do no harm to the public.
- A business is expected to take responsibility for its effect on consumers and society in general and conduct itself ethically and morally, which includes accounting for global humanitarian rights issues.
- **Social responsibility** refers to a company's acceptance of the role that ethics play in its business and its obligations to consider consumer and societal well-being in relation to the company's performance and profits.
- The three main global responsibilities of a business include (1) a **moral duty for humanitarian rights**, (2) **protection and sustainability of the environment**, and (3) a **duty to provide a return on shareholders' investments**.
- Sustainable business growth and responsibility involves a company recognizing their duty to be socially responsible and ethical in the areas of company growth, profits, and employee well-being. This is also known as the **three Ps—people, planet,** and **profit.**
- The **public interest theory of regulation** argues that government intervention in markets is needed as a response to market failures and imperfections.
- The **business interest theory of regulation** says that government should intervene to ensure fair competition.
- Government regulation of business is based not only on real ethical issues, but also perceived ethical issues. The three most significant ethical challenges encountered in the workplace are (1) conflicts of interest, (2) accountability, and (3) honesty and integrity.
- Employers have a duty to safeguard employees' personal information, eliminate discrimination and sexual harassment, and carry out their duties to achieve the best interests of the corporation and shareholders.

- **Whistleblowing** is when an employee discloses to company executives, to government representatives, or to the media the illegal or unethical practices that are being committed by the company.
- **Discrimination** in the workplace is the negative treatment of a job candidate or an employee due to bias. Legally, such bias occurs on the basis of race, color, religion, sex (including pregnancy, sexual orientation, or gender identity), national origin, age, disability, and genetic information (including family medical history).
- **Sexism** occurs when individuals are treated differently based on gender. Sexism can become discrimination when it occurs in the workplace.
  - **Sex discrimination** involves work-related decisions based on gender.
  - **Sexual harassment** refers to work-related decisions that specifically are based on unwelcome sexual advances or inappropriate sexual remarks.
- Corporate officers have moral obligations to exercise due diligence in actions on behalf of the corporation and reasonable prudence in carrying out their duties to achieve the best interests of the corporation, in addition to fiduciary duties to shareholders. These moral obligations are not only to shareholders but also to employees, with the biggest obligation to ensure the health and safety of the employees.
- A **union** is a group of workers, not necessarily from the same company, who band together to achieve common goals in the areas of wages, hours, and working conditions, such as the use of child labor. A **union contract** is a formal agreement between a company's management and its employees that serves as a guide to their relationship, with the rights of each party clearly spelled out.
- A business has a moral obligation to use ethical practices in marketing and advertising, refrain from corporate spying, and protect its employees' and consumers' privacy.
- **Cybersecurity** is the state of being protected against the criminal or unauthorized use of electronic data. It is classified into five types of protection: (1) critical infrastructure security, (2) application security, (3) network security, (4) cloud security, and (5) internet of things (IoT) security. Businesses have an ethical duty to implement a cybersecurity model that protects confidentiality, integrity, and availability.
- Information technology regulations are outdated. However, consumers have the right to be protected from unfair business practices. It is a corporation's duty to ensure that the rights of consumers are protected, and they are informed of any ethical breaches.
- **Global corporate citizenship** refers to a corporation's legal and political responsibilities for operating in a global economy.

- The United Nations **Global Compact** is a corporate citizen network created to promote world-wide corporate responsibility while being sensitive to the world's various cultural norms.
- **Outsourcing** involves using vendors for goods or services previously handled in-house or in-country. **Offshoring** is about relocation of business processes always outside of the country in which the company resides. Both involve various ethical concerns, such as the use of sweat shops, child labor, or slave labor, as well as fair trade laws and standards.

Chapter 4

Business Ethics and Society Post-Test

POST-TEST ANSWER SHEET

1. Ⓐ Ⓑ Ⓒ Ⓓ	14. Ⓐ Ⓑ Ⓒ Ⓓ	27. Ⓐ Ⓑ Ⓒ Ⓓ
2. Ⓐ Ⓑ Ⓒ Ⓓ	15. Ⓐ Ⓑ Ⓒ Ⓓ	28. Ⓐ Ⓑ Ⓒ Ⓓ
3. Ⓐ Ⓑ Ⓒ Ⓓ	16. Ⓐ Ⓑ Ⓒ Ⓓ	29. Ⓐ Ⓑ Ⓒ Ⓓ
4. Ⓐ Ⓑ Ⓒ Ⓓ	17. Ⓐ Ⓑ Ⓒ Ⓓ	30. Ⓐ Ⓑ Ⓒ Ⓓ
5. Ⓐ Ⓑ Ⓒ Ⓓ	18. Ⓐ Ⓑ Ⓒ Ⓓ	31. Ⓐ Ⓑ Ⓒ Ⓓ
6. Ⓐ Ⓑ Ⓒ Ⓓ	19. Ⓐ Ⓑ Ⓒ Ⓓ	32. Ⓐ Ⓑ Ⓒ Ⓓ
7. Ⓐ Ⓑ Ⓒ Ⓓ	20. Ⓐ Ⓑ Ⓒ Ⓓ	33. Ⓐ Ⓑ Ⓒ Ⓓ
8. Ⓐ Ⓑ Ⓒ Ⓓ	21. Ⓐ Ⓑ Ⓒ Ⓓ	34. Ⓐ Ⓑ Ⓒ Ⓓ
9. Ⓐ Ⓑ Ⓒ Ⓓ	22. Ⓐ Ⓑ Ⓒ Ⓓ	35. Ⓐ Ⓑ Ⓒ Ⓓ
10. Ⓐ Ⓑ Ⓒ Ⓓ	23. Ⓐ Ⓑ Ⓒ Ⓓ	36. Ⓐ Ⓑ Ⓒ Ⓓ
11. Ⓐ Ⓑ Ⓒ Ⓓ	24. Ⓐ Ⓑ Ⓒ Ⓓ	37. Ⓐ Ⓑ Ⓒ Ⓓ
12. Ⓐ Ⓑ Ⓒ Ⓓ	25. Ⓐ Ⓑ Ⓒ Ⓓ	38. Ⓐ Ⓑ Ⓒ Ⓓ
13. Ⓐ Ⓑ Ⓒ Ⓓ	26. Ⓐ Ⓑ Ⓒ Ⓓ	39. Ⓐ Ⓑ Ⓒ Ⓓ

40. Ⓐ Ⓑ Ⓒ Ⓓ   47. Ⓐ Ⓑ Ⓒ Ⓓ   54. Ⓐ Ⓑ Ⓒ Ⓓ

41. Ⓐ Ⓑ Ⓒ Ⓓ   48. Ⓐ Ⓑ Ⓒ Ⓓ   55. Ⓐ Ⓑ Ⓒ Ⓓ

42. Ⓐ Ⓑ Ⓒ Ⓓ   49. Ⓐ Ⓑ Ⓒ Ⓓ   56. Ⓐ Ⓑ Ⓒ Ⓓ

43. Ⓐ Ⓑ Ⓒ Ⓓ   50. Ⓐ Ⓑ Ⓒ Ⓓ   57. Ⓐ Ⓑ Ⓒ Ⓓ

44. Ⓐ Ⓑ Ⓒ Ⓓ   51. Ⓐ Ⓑ Ⓒ Ⓓ   58. Ⓐ Ⓑ Ⓒ Ⓓ

45. Ⓐ Ⓑ Ⓒ Ⓓ   52. Ⓐ Ⓑ Ⓒ Ⓓ   59. Ⓐ Ⓑ Ⓒ Ⓓ

46. Ⓐ Ⓑ Ⓒ Ⓓ   53. Ⓐ Ⓑ Ⓒ Ⓓ   60. Ⓐ Ⓑ Ⓒ Ⓓ

BUSINESS ETHICS AND SOCIETY POST-TEST
72 minutes—60 questions

Directions: Carefully read each of the following 60 questions. Choose the best answer to each question and fill in the corresponding circle on the answer sheet. The Answer Key and Explanations can be found following this post-test.

1. Which federal act, as a result of multiple scandals and frauds, created enhanced financial statement disclosures, established criminal penalties for CEOs and CFOs who defraud investors, put in place safeguards for whistleblowers, and established a new regulatory body for public accounting firms?

   A. Fair Labor Standards Act
   B. Sarbanes-Oxley Act
   C. Taft-Hartley Act
   D. Whistleblower Act

2. Which of the following statements about fair trade laws is not true?

   A. Fair trade laws started as a group of state laws that resulted in the Miller-Tydings Act to exempt fair trade from antitrust laws.
   B. Fair trade laws originally permitted manufacturers to set a minimum retail price on a product.
   C. International fair trade laws allow governments to offset subsidies through lower import duties.
   D. International fair trade laws allow governments to offset subsidies through higher import duties.

3. What are tacit expectations that exist between employers and employees called?

   A. Psychological contracts
   B. Social contracts
   C. Employment agreements
   D. Human resource letters of expectations

4. When it comes to proprietary information on computer networks, what are the two types of general security threats that exist?

   A. Hackers and Trojan horses
   B. Phishing and malware
   C. E-crime and malware
   D. E-crime and Trojan horses

5. What is a defining feature of a transnational company?

   A. A company that has a strong national identification
   B. A company with one sole owner
   C. A publicly held company
   D. A company that has no identifiable home country base

6. What essentially do whistleblower laws protect the whistleblower against?

   A. Legal liability
   B. Retaliation
   C. Punitive damages
   D. Indemnity

7. What is the moral dilemma a company faces when deciding whether to take on a moral or political stance, such as Nike did with its Colin Kaepernick ad?

   A. Choosing between social responsibility and duty to shareholders
   B. Choosing between self-expression and profits
   C. Choosing between employees' opinions and community opinions
   D. Choosing between corporate officers' beliefs and employees' beliefs

8. In what year did the FCC start allowing a single company to own both types of media within the same market?

   A. 2003
   B. 2010
   C. 2017
   D. 2020

9. Which of the following best defines slave labor?

    A. Workers who are paid what is called a nonliving wage
    B. Workers who are coerced into working for a woefully inadequate reward
    C. Workers who are involved in production and manufacturing
    D. Workers who earn a minimum wage

10. Social contract theories say that a company has a social responsibility to the community to which it belongs because

    A. the company and community have a co-dependency and therefore follow tacit rules.
    B. government does not adequately provide for communities.
    C. shareholders are most interested in society's well-being.
    D. communities are dependent on businesses.

11. Issues that have arisen as a result of marketing departments mining social media for data include which of the following?

    A. Targeting capabilities of the web, government supervision, false information, and marketing techniques
    B. Government supervision, false information, marketing techniques, and ownership of the web
    C. Ownership of web user data, targeting capabilities of the web, government supervision, and privacy
    D. False information, marketing techniques, ownership of the web, and government supervision

12. What are the three main global responsibilities that an international corporation has?

    A. A moral duty for humanitarian rights, sustainability of resources, and a duty to provide a return on shareholders' investments
    B. A moral duty for humanitarian rights, protection and sustainability of the environment, and a duty to provide a return on shareholders' investments
    C. A moral duty of humanitarian rights, sustainability of resources, and a duty to meet shareholders' demands
    D. A moral duty of humanitarian rights, protection and sustainability of the environment, and protection of workers' rights

13. What is the specific term used for a company's effort to contribute through cash, time, or product to the communities in which it earns its profits, that results in higher employee morale, enhanced company image, and improved customer relations?

    A. Corporate responsibility
    B. Socialism
    C. Corporate philanthropy
    D. Corporate obligation

14. Why is ethical leadership at the top of any company so important?

    A. It sets the tone for ethical behavior throughout the organization.
    B. It indicates that top management makes the most money.
    C. It indicates that top management has the most responsibility within the organization.
    D. It provides communities and stakeholders with a positive image of the organization.

15. Which of the following is the term that is used when government has little or no involvement in regulating business?

    A. Deregulator government
    B. Free enterprise system
    C. Mixed enterprise system
    D. Laissez-faire government

16. What marketing practice targets ads to certain specific groups?

    A. Pricing strategy
    B. Skimming
    C. Selective marketing
    D. Shilling

17. In addition to trying to create fair competition between domestic and foreign countries, fair trade is also a way to

    A. promote national isolationism.
    B. raise standards of living in developing countries.
    C. create more opportunities for domestic producers.
    D. create more opportunities for foreign producers.

18. Which of the following is the term used for the state of being protected against the criminal or unauthorized use of electronic data?

A. Intelligent fact-finding
B. Data protection
C. Internet security
D. Cybersecurity

19. Which of the following is NOT a term for the practice of using espionage techniques for commercial or financial purposes?

A. Corporate spying
B. Defense spying
C. Industrial espionage
D. Economic espionage

20. Sexual harassment in the workplace is concerned with questions of what is acceptable and unacceptable within the workplace from the perspective of

I. the receiver.
II. the initiator.
III. gender.

A. I only
B. II only
C. I and II
D. I, II, and III

21. Who developed the theory on moral development that indicates individuals develop moral standards in six different stages that can be grouped into three levels of development?

A. Lawrence Kohlberg
B. Carol Gilligan
C. James R. Rest
D. Thomas Hobbes

22. Based on what theory is crossing a striker's picket line by a union worker considered unethical?

    A. Theory of egoism
    B. Deontology theory of ethics
    C. Social contract theory
    D. Theory of relativism

23. The right to be safe, the right to be informed, the right to choose, and the right to be heard are a part of

    A. employee rights.
    B. consumer rights.
    C. shareholder rights.
    D. vendor rights.

24. What duty to employees does an employer have regarding employee confidential data?

    A. To establish processes to safeguard sensitive employee data
    B. To establish processes to safeguard sensitive employee data and to notify employees of any type of breach to that data
    C. To prevent breaches to sensitive employee data through cybersecurity
    D. To prevent breaches to sensitive employee data through cyber-security and to notify employees of any type of breach to that data

25. What is another name for business ethics?

    A. Corporate social responsibility
    B. Corporate philanthropy
    C. Business morals
    D. Business culture

26. Prior to a Supreme Court ruling in June 2020, Title VII of the Civil Rights Act of 1964 did NOT prohibit discrimination on the basis of

    A. race.
    B. sexual orientation.
    C. religious affiliation.
    D. age.

27. What is a legal method that some companies employ to get around the Foreign Corrupt Practices Act of 1977?

A. Licensing a company in a foreign country
B. Offshoring to a foreign country
C. Outsourcing to a foreign country
D. Bribing a nongovernment official

28. Which federal act requires most companies with 100 or more employees to notify those employees and the community 60 calendar days in advance of a closing or massive layoff?

A. Sarbanes-Oxley Act of 2002
B. Family and Medical Leave Act of 1993
C. Equal Pay Act of 1963
D. Worker Adjustment and Retraining Notification Act of 1988

29. A business must be which of the following to be sustainable?

A. Profit-seeking, shareholder-focused, and employee-friendly
B. Branded, cost-centered, and people-focused
C. Economically viable, socially responsible, and environmentally friendly
D. Energy-efficient, cost-centered, and people-focused

30. Under which of the following situations is an employer NOT allowed to dismiss an employee when the company is located within an at-will state?

A. The employee's performance is outstanding.
B. The employee is underperforming.
C. The company is downsizing.
D. The company is dismissing anyone over the age of 65.

31. Which of the following examples is a form of deceptive advertising not allowed by the FTC?

    A. A commercial in which two women are talking, and one of them purports a special feature of a product, and the other woman expresses that her product doesn't have the feature

    B. An announcer in a commercial who is not familiar to consumers talks about the abilities of a particular medical product to relieve pain

    C. A celebrity in a commercial who has not used a product implies that they have used it

    D. A company takes an excerpt from a critic's review and places that review without alterations into its ad

32. Who is personally liable for the debts of a corporation if the business does not have enough funds to cover the debt?

    A. CEO
    B. Board of Directors
    C. Shareholders
    D. No one

33. What moral philosophy is in play when bribery is viewed as a normal way of doing business within a particular country?

    A. Relativism
    B. Utilitarianism
    C. Egoism
    D. Deontology

34. Which of the following is NOT considered to be proprietary information?

    A. Trade secrets
    B. Intellectual property
    C. Patents
    D. Formulas

35. What is defined as the values and norms, global in nature, that concern world poverty, environmental problems, peace and security, and human rights?

A. Utilitarian ethics
B. Global ethics
C. Relativism
D. Domestic ethics

36. A nondisclosure agreement is intended to

A. reveal conflicts of interest.
B. protect an employee's confidential data.
C. protect an employee's privacy.
D. protect proprietary information.

37. Which of the following statements is TRUE regarding whistleblowing?

A. Whistleblowing is appropriate when an employee sees any type of perceived infraction by corporate officials.
B. Whistleblowing is inappropriate if the employee does not first discuss the infraction with a supervisor.
C. Even if a confidentiality agreement has been signed by an employee, an employee may disclose confidential information if it is for the purpose of disclosing illegal, immoral, or unethical practices committed by the company.
D. If a confidentiality agreement has been signed by an employee, an employee may not disclose any confidential information under any circumstance.

38. Which of the following is NOT an example of a business conflict of interest?

A. An employee is married to their supervisor's boss.
B. An employee with a noncompete agreement starts a company that provides the same type of services as their full-time employer.
C. An employee who is on a hiring committee does not disclose that they are related to a job candidate.
D. An individual provides leadership training for the company on whose board they serve, and they receive a fee for the service.

39. What do all companies, whether small or large, have in common?

      I. An economic impact on a country

      II. The ability to meet the wants and needs of a society

      III. An impact on innovation and new inventions

A. I only
B. III only
C. I and II only
D. I and III only

40. Why does a highly developed country allow other countries to import goods?

A. As a gesture of social responsibility and a means of obtaining lower-priced goods
B. As a means of obtaining lower-priced goods and to meet domestic wants and needs
C. As a means of obtaining lower-priced goods, to meet domestic wants and needs, and to establish good will with other nations
D. To meet domestic wants and needs

41. Which of the following is viewed as morally acceptable spying software?

A. Software that secretly tracks communications between two different networks to obtain confidential information
B. Software that allows a company to filter access to particular sites on all of its company computers
C. Software tracking pixels that secretly allow a company to see whether one has opened an email from the company, how long it took for the email to be read, and how often an individual returns to read the email, in order sell information to marketing companies
D. Software that covertly gathers information about an organization and is then sold to marketing companies

42. Which of the following actions is an example of an employer not fulfilling its responsibility for workplace safety?

A. A supervisor does not submit a reprimand when a newer window washer employee forgets to fasten their safety harness.

B. A company does not provide escorts to employees' cars, even though the area where some employees park has seen an uptick in crime.

C. An employer declines to move an employee with severe allergic reactions to spores in the air to a different office because the levels of spores in the air at the current office space tested below acceptable levels.

D. A company installs the minimum number of smoke detectors as called for by OSHA and local coding regulations.

43. Which of the following is the theory that argues for government intervention in markets as a response to market failures and imperfections in order to promote general welfare rather than the interests of influential stakeholders?

A. Public interest theory of regulation

B. Business interest theory of regulation

C. Government interest theory of regulation

D. Political interest theory of regulation

44. Which of the following statements about social responsibility is accurate?

A. Social responsibility does not provide corporate advantage.

B. Social responsibility does not provide for workers' well-being.

C. Social responsibility is unquestionably morally superior to a business's need to make a profit.

D. Social responsibility is just one aspect of business ethics.

45. Which of the following is considered a moral issue with some product warranties?

A. The warranties are limited.

B. The warranties are intended to obtain consumer information rather than to financially protect the customer against issues of defect.

C. The warranties may cost the consumer shipping and handling fees.

D. The warranties are not honored, and the consumer has no recourse.

46. A top-level company officer fails to convince the board of directors that the company should not build on a particular site because of an environmental concern. This officer quits their high-paying position and proceeds to develop a new company whose mission is to protect the environment at all costs, which includes boycotting the former company. In what level of moral development is this corporate officer in?

A. Pre-conventional
B. Conventional
C. Post-conventional
D. Individualism

47. What is the moral argument for trade agreements?

A. Even if one country is economically better off than the other countries involved, there is a mutually beneficial relationship.
B. Even if one country is economically better off than the other countries involved, the other countries are being socially responsible on a more global basis.
C. Trade agreements are more beneficial for some countries than for others.
D. Trade agreements create obstacles for countries not involved in the agreements.

48. What is defined as negative treatment of a job candidate or employee due to bias?

A. Favoritism
B. Discrimination
C. Equal opportunity
D. Partiality

49. Upon which of the following theories is global responsibility based?

A. Relativism
B. Egoism
C. Social contract
D. Utilitarianism

50. Which of the following is TRUE regarding corporations and their employees?

    A. A socially responsible corporation will pay its employees a living wage whenever possible.

    B. A socially responsible corporation will start by paying minimum wage and then slowly increase the wage to as much as possible.

    C. In return for receiving wages, employees owe a company loyalty unless the employee decides to move on to another company.

    D. In return for receiving wages, employees owe a company only honesty.

51. Which of the following terms refers to a company's acceptance of the role that ethics play in its business and a company's obligations to consider consumer and societal well-being in relation to the company's performance and profits?

    A. Legal responsibility

    B. Environmental responsibility

    C. Lobbying responsibility

    D. Social responsibility

52. Under the Foreign Corrupt Practices Act of 1977, companies are allowed to do which one of the following?

    A. Pay a foreign government official with a lavish gift to obtain a permit to set up a business in a country where bribery is a normal custom.

    B. Lobby politicians in both the US and in foreign governments to try to affect legislation.

    C. Pay a foreign official's friend with cash to obtain a permit to build a new office.

    D. Pay a judge in a foreign court to release employees who were caught disobeying the law.

53. Under which of the following conditions is an employer allowed to invade an employee's expectation of privacy by recording phone calls?

    A. If an employer suspects the employee of wrongdoing, and the employer is investigating the employee's phone activity to catch the employee in the act
    B. If an employer wants to monitor phone conversations for quality assurance purposes
    C. If an employer wants to monitor phone conversations for quality assurance purposes, and the employer notifies all parties who will be recorded
    D. If an employer is investigating an employee because there is evidence of fraud

54. Which of the following is a social, not legal, responsibility that a company has to its employees?

    A. Health insurance
    B. Life insurance
    C. Flexible work schedule
    D. Quality of life benefits

55. What is the term that describes a group of workers who have banded together to achieve common goals in the areas of wages, hours, and working conditions?

    A. Mediator
    B. Union
    C. Arbitrator
    D. Striker

56. Which Maslow's Hierarchy of Needs theory coincides with Kohlberg's highest level of moral development?

    A. Physiological needs
    B. Safety needs
    C. Social needs
    D. Esteem needs

57. In terms of legality, sexual harassment

   A. only involves unwelcome advances of a sexual nature in the workplace.
   B. is the same as sex discrimination.
   C. involves unwelcome and inappropriate actions of a sexual nature in the workplace.
   D. involves unwelcome and inappropriate actions of a sexual nature in the workplace and in public.

58. On what philosophical theory is an employee's actions based if an employee who routinely travels for business uses reward points they have earned from work-related hotel stays for a personal vacation?

   A. Egoism
   B. Utilitarianism
   C. Relativism
   D. Deontology

59. Which of the following is a FALSE statement regarding a corporation's relationship with stockholders?

   A. A corporation's fiduciary duty to stockholders involves doing anything to grow profits.
   B. A corporation has a duty to stockholders to make a profit.
   C. A corporation has a duty to fulfill its social responsibility, especially if its mission is based on such responsibility.
   D. A corporation has a duty to its stockholders to protect the company's employees from injury.

60. Which of the following best describes why the Uniformed Services Employment Rights Act of 1993 was enacted?

   A. The act was created solely to protect the rights of veterans.
   B. The act was created to hold companies accountable for their patriotic duty.
   C. The act was created to prevent employment discrimination on the basis of membership in or obligation to serve in the uniformed services.
   D. The act was created to help disabled veterans.

ANSWER KEY AND EXPLANATIONS

1. B	13. C	25. C	37. C	49. D
2. C	14. A	26. B	38. D	50. A
3. A	15. D	27. A	39. C	51. D
4. C	16. C	28. D	40. C	52. B
5. D	17. B	29. C	41. B	53. C
6. B	18. D	30. D	42. A	54. D
7. A	19. B	31. C	43. A	55. B
8. C	20. A	32. D	44. D	56. D
9. B	21. A	33. A	45. B	57. C
10. A	22. C	34. C	46. C	58. A
11. C	23. B	35. B	47. A	59. A
12. B	24. B	36. D	48. B	60. C

1. **The correct answer is B.** The Sarbanes-Oxley Act of 2002 came about because of frauds perpetrated by corporation officers at WorldCom and Enron due to lack of public oversight. The Fair Labor Standards Act (choice A) set the first minimum wage and banned child labor. The Taft-Hartley Act (choice C) limited unions' power in trying to build up memberships. There is no such piece of legislation called the Whistleblower Act (choice D) even though the Sarbanes-Oxley Act is sometimes referred to as such.

2. **The correct answer is C.** This statement is false because governments offset subsidies by setting higher import duties, not lower ones. To avoid foreign companies from dumping their goods at extremely low prices, governments will step in and increase import duties to offset any subsidy the foreign company may have received.

3. **The correct answer is A.** A psychological contract in the workplace is tacit knowledge that exists in an employment relationship. It is neither a written contract nor an oral agreement, but rather an implicit or tacit understanding. For example, an employer can expect that an employee will be at work on time, and the employee can expect to get paid on time. A social contract (choice B) is what exists between individuals living in a community or society. Employment agreements (choice C) and letters of expectations (choice D) are explicit, not tacit.

4. **The correct answer is C.** E-crime and malware are the two types of general security threats to proprietary information on computer networks. A hacker is a name for someone who commits e-crime. A Trojan horse is a type of malware. Phishing is the name of a type of social engineering used to acquire sensitive information.

5. **The correct answer is D.** Transnational corporations are companies that have no identifiable home country base. These corporations are interested in most markets; they do not focus only on the market in a specific country. As such, they are not controlled by nationals of any specific country.

6. **The correct answer is B.** Whistleblower laws protect individuals from retaliation for having exposed wrongdoing. Legal liability (choice A) is incorrect because whistleblower laws do not protect whistleblowing individuals from legal liability since they may have also had a hand in the wrongdoing. Choice C is incorrect because punitive damages would be found against the organization's officers, not the whistleblower. *Indemnity* (choice D) is another word for punitive damages.

7. **The correct answer is A.** A moral dilemma involves making a difficult choice between two courses of action, either of which will go against a moral principle if not chosen. In the example with Nike, the company was faced with the moral dilemma of whether to not act in a socially responsible way or not to be concerned with its duty to shareholders to provide profits. Choice B is incorrect because a company does not have self-expression, and profits by themselves are not a moral principle. There are no moral principles or obligations involved in choices C and D.

8. **The correct answer is C.** In 2017, the FCC started allowing a single company to own both types of media within the same market. Prior to 2017, the FCC enforced rules prohibiting monopolies in news communication. No single company was allowed to own both a television station and a newspaper in the same market area.

9. **The correct answer is B.** Workers in many foreign countries are forced into working long hours for little to no wages in order to have minimum shelter. This is a woefully inadequate reward for their labor. Choice A is not the best answer because there is much debate as to what constitutes a living wage. Choice C is incorrect because not all workers in manufacturing and production are slave laborers, even though it is often in these areas that slave labor occurs. Choice D is incorrect because a minimum wage is deemed to be an adequate reward for the work produced.

10. **The correct answer is A.** A community is dependent upon businesses to employ its citizens, and businesses are dependent upon their communities to provide workers. This economic dependency forms a tacit agreement between the two where the company should perform in such a way to help provide for community needs. Choice B is incorrect because governments provide for communities in differing amounts. The social contract in this case is between the government and the community. Choice C is incorrect because not all shareholders hold the same reason for their investments. Many shareholders are strictly interested in their investments' growth. Choice D is incorrect because communities are co-dependent, not just dependent.

11. **The correct answer is C.** Data mining by companies has resulted in concerns over who the information really belongs to, the ability to target vulnerable groups such as teens, how much government intervention should be put in place, and privacy of consumer information. Choices A, B, and D include factors that have nothing to do with the data mining and do not contain the key concern about privacy.

12. **The correct answer is B.** Companies that are globally responsible believe in a moral duty regarding the rights of all humans—employees, shareholders, communities, etc. Such companies also believe in both protecting the environment and sustaining the environment's resources, as well as working toward a return on shareholders' investments. Choice A does not include protection of the environment, such as the dumping of chemicals into the water. It only focuses on sustaining resources such as energy. Choice C is incorrect because a company does not have an obligation to meet shareholders' demands, as these may be unrealistic or even unethical. Choice D does not include the duty to shareholders, and the protection of workers' rights would fall under humanitarian rights.

13. **The correct answer is C.** Corporate philanthropy can involve the donation of cash, support of employees' time to volunteer their efforts, etc., to provide for the public good of its communities. Corporate responsibility (choice A) includes much more than just corporate philanthropy, such as in efforts to protect the environment. Socialism (choice B) is a form of economic system in which the government owns the major industries. Choice D is incorrect because corporations are not obliged to donate anything.

14. **The correct answer is A.** When there is ethical leadership at the top of a company, it demonstrates the expected behavior for everyone in the company to follow. In other words, ethical leadership sets the tone for the company. Ethical leadership has nothing to do with how much money top management makes or the responsibilities of top management, so choices B and C cannot be correct. Similarly, while choice D may be true, it has nothing to do with why ethical leadership is important.

15. The correct answer is D. *Laissez faire* is a French term meaning "not to be involved." Some argue that government should not be involved (laissez faire), while others argue that government regulation ensures safety and fair competition. Choice A is incorrect because deregulation is not a type of government but rather is what a government does when it opens up competition in particular industries. A free enterprise system (choice B) is an economic system that allows for private ownership of businesses. A mixed enterprise system (choice C) is an economic system in which there is both private and public ownership of businesses.

16. The correct answer is C. Selective marketing is where marketing departments target their advertising to certain select groups. This practice raises ethical questions as to who may be included (and excluded) from product knowledge.

17. The correct answer is B. Usually we think of fair trade as a means of ensuring other countries do not export goods at such a low price that domestic companies cannot compete. However, fair trade also includes providing an opportunity for goods produced by refugees and other disadvantaged groups so that their quality of life improves. Choice A is incorrect because fair trade does the opposite of isolating a country. Choices C and D are incorrect because fair trade is not about creating more opportunities domestically or internationally, but rather ensuring equal opportunity for domestic and foreign companies.

18. The correct answer is D. Cybersecurity is the term used to denote the state of being protected against the criminal or unauthorized use of electronic data. Intelligent fact-finding (choice A) is when a company wants to uncover information about a client by analyzing public records and surveying a competitor's clients. Fact-finding is ethical when a company clearly identifies itself and its purpose. It is unethical when a company extracts information through backdoor encryption technology. Data protection (choice B) and internet security (choice C) are important parts of cybersecurity.

19. **The correct answer is B.** Defense spying is a type of espionage in which governmental secrets are involved. Corporate spying (choice A) is a term used to describe illegally obtaining another company's trade secrets. Industrial espionage (choice C) involves commercial production secrets. Economic espionage (choice D) is what happens when one company spies on another, seeking unethical financial gain.

20. **The correct answer is A.** Sexual harassment is considered from the perspective of the receiver. In other words, the harassment is assessed from the perspective of the individual who is on the receiving end of unwelcome sexual advances. While gender is certainly a factor, it is not the deciding factor in whether the sexual advances or conduct are considered harassment.

21. **The correct answer is A.** Lawrence Kohlberg was the first to develop a theory based on research with children as to how moral behavior evolves through three different levels of development—pre-conventional, conventional, and post-conventional. Carol Gilligan (choice B) created the theory of women's moral development. While Kohlberg's theory was more justice-oriented, Gilligan's was care-oriented. Rest (choice C) further developed Kohlberg's theory (neo-Kohlbergian approach). James R. Rest's theory views moral development as being more fluid. Thomas Hobbes (choice D) created the social contract theory, which says behavior is based on the norms of a society.

22. **The correct answer is C.** The social contract theory is based on the idea that individuals tacitly accept the rules and morals of a society simply by remaining in that society. In this case, a union worker explicitly accepts the rules set forth by the union, which does not allow crossing the picket line. The theory of egoism (choice A) would actually provide support for the action as being ethical if it is in the best interest of the worker. The deontology theory of ethics (choice B) says that the action itself is right or wrong, but as is shown, the action may be considered right under some circumstances and wrong under others. The theory of relativism (choice D) is based on the norm of one's culture. Some cultures find crossing the picket line acceptable, whereas others do not.

23. **The correct answer is B.** The right to be safe, the right to be informed, the right to choose, and the right to be heard are a part of consumer rights. Employees (choice A) do not have the right to be informed or to be heard. Employers have the duty to employees to keep employees safe, and employees have the right to choose where they work. Shareholder safety (choice C) does not come into question, so the right is meaningless. Vendors (choice D) do not have the right to be informed if a company decides to stop using their services.

24. **The correct answer is B.** An employer has a duty to both develop safeguarding processes and to inform employees if there has been a breach to the information. Choice A only includes one of the employer's duties. Choices C and D are incorrect because not all breaches occur through cyberspace. For example, not securing paper files with employee information would violate the employer's duty.

25. **The correct answer is C.** Business ethics is also known as business morals. Choice A is not the best answer because corporate social responsibility is one way in which a company can be ethical. Corporate philanthropy (choice B) is a specific type of corporate social responsibility. A business's culture (choice D) can be ethical or unethical.

26. **The correct answer is B.** Title VII of the Civil Rights Act prohibited discrimination on the basis of sex (meaning gender), but the original law and the 1991 expansion of this act did not address discrimination on the basis of sexual orientation. In *Bostock v. Clayton County*, the US Supreme Court ruled that sex discrimination includes discrimination against sexual orientation or transgender status.

27. **The correct answer is A.** By licensing a foreign company, a domestic company effectively gives the foreign company its revenues less a royalty fee that the domestic company gets. Hence, the foreign company then uses some of the revenue to pay off government officials. Choice B is incorrect because offshoring is simply a domestic country paying a foreign business to produce part of its product without using bribery. Choice C is incorrect because outsourcing to a foreign company is the same as offshoring. Choice D is incorrect because, even though the law does not allow a domestic company to bribe a government official, the law also does not allow the bribery of a government representative, a type of nongovernment official.

28. **The correct answer is D.** The Worker Adjustment and Retraining Notification Act of 1988 (WARN) was intended to protect employees and their families from totally unexpected unemployment and to provide the community with an economic warning. The Sarbanes-Oxley Act of 2002 (choice A) was enacted to hold corporate officers more accountable for accurate financial information. The Family and Medical Leave Act of 1993 (choice B) requires companies of 50 or employees to provide 12 weeks of unpaid leave for the birth of a child, adoption, becoming a foster parent, or when caring for a seriously ill spouse or relative. The Equal Pay Act of 1963 (choice C) requires equal pay for equal efforts.

29. **The correct answer is C.** For a business to be sustainable, it must be economically viable (meaning the company has enough money to continue its business), socially responsible, and environmentally friendly. Choice A is incorrect because profit seeking does not necessarily make a company economically viable. Also, the focus in this answer choice is only on shareholders and employees, not the rest of stakeholders. Choice B is incorrect because *branded* simply means that individuals are aware of a company; however, this awareness alone does not make a company viable. Also, if a company is too cost-centered, it usually indicates issues with profits. Choice D is incorrect because energy efficiency is only one aspect of being environmentally friendly.

30. **The correct answer is D.** Employers are not allowed to dismiss employees on the basis of discrimination, even in an at-will state. In this case, age discrimination is at work.

31. **The correct answer is C.** The FTC does not allow endorsements of a product, even implied ones, if the individual has never used the product and the public would be swayed to use the product because of the individual endorsing the product. The example in choice A is not considered an endorsement; it is expected that the average person would understand the situation. Choice B is incorrect because the announcer is not considered an influencer since they are unknown. Choice D is incorrect because the critic's review is a public statement and as long as there is no alteration of that excerpt, the FTC allows it.

32. **The correct answer is D.** Because a corporation is a legal entity, only the business's assets can be used to pay its debt or legal fines. If there are not enough assets to cover the debt, then creditors do not get paid. The individuals in choices A, B, and C are not personally liable for a corporation's debt.

33. **The correct answer is A.** The ethical theory of relativism is based on the idea that morality is relative to cultural norms. In this case, the cultural norm is bribery. Utilitarianism (choice B) is based on the idea of the greatest good. Egoism (choice C) is based on self-interest rather than cultural norms. Deontology (choice D) emphasizes duty as a part of morality.

34. **The correct answer is C.** Patents on products or services are public information. Trade secrets, intellectual property, and formulas are considered private, proprietary information.

35. **The correct answer is B.** Global ethics is the set of values and norms that are developing on a worldwide basis. While utilitarian ethics (choice A) is based on the idea of the greatest good, it is not based on the idea of community. Global ethics is based on the idea of the world being one community. Relativism (choice C) is based on culture. Domestic ethics (choice D) indicates ethics not based on globalization.

36. The correct answer is D. One way to protect a company's proprietary information is to have contracts with those employees and vendors who know the information, requiring them not to disclose it. Conflicts of interest (choice A) are handled through conflict-of-interest disclosure agreements. Choice B is incorrect because even though nondisclosure agreements are also known as confidentiality agreements, the intent of these agreements is to protect employer information, not employee information. Choice C is incorrect because an employer has a duty to respect an employee's privacy to an extent.

37. The correct answer is C. The protection afforded under the Sarbanes-Oxley Act allows an employee to break a confidentiality agreement if that employee has discovered such wrongdoing and discloses that information to company officials, government authorities, or the media. Choice A is incorrect because some infractions may be based upon a perception rather than reality; in those cases, whistleblowing may not be appropriate. An example of this is an employee who discloses the company's secret formula because it contains a chemical that changes color during the processing. Choice B is incorrect because Sarbanes-Oxley protects employees who may be afraid to approach company officials. Sarbanes-Oxley allows for the situation in choice D.

38. The correct answer is D. A board member can do business for the company they serve and receive a fee without there being a conflict of interest. A conflict would arise if that board member did not disclose that they do this type of work for the company's competitors. There is a direct conflict of interest in choice A; the supervisor will find it difficult to reprimand the spouse if needed because doing so could affect the supervisor's performance review. A conflict of interest exists in choice B, as the employee is now directly competing with the employer. Choice C is also a conflict of interest; one would expect the employee to act more favorably toward a relative.

39. The correct answer is C. No matter what the size, a company can have either a positive or negative economic effect on a country. Even small businesses pay taxes and use other vendors who in return have an economic impact. Companies also have the ability to meet the wants and needs of a society, whether through its products and services or through the mission it carries out. However, not all businesses impact innovation. Certain products become obsolete or cannot be repurposed. A good example of this is the television set with vacuum tubes. Once such tubes became obsolete, some businesses continued to produce rather than innovate.

40. The correct answer is C. Countries such as the United States, even though highly developed, seek to obtain lower-priced goods both to satisfy domestic consumers and to create fair competition, which leads to innovation. In addition, allowing some imports from countries where there have been strained relations provides an opening for the two countries to establish a better relationship. Choice A is incorrect because one government does not have a social responsibility to another government. Choices B and D are both missing one of the three factors mentioned in choice C.

41. The correct answer is B. A company is allowed to use filtering software as it is on company property, and it does not affect employee privacy. The software described in choices A, B, and D is secretive in nature; the intention is either to obtain confidential information or to sell confidential information.

42. The correct answer is A. Regardless of the length of employment, an employer has a duty to ensure the safety of workers as well as customers. In this case, failing to reprimand the employee on such an infraction, even if the supervisor views their own actions as being kind to the employee, could lead to the employee's continued carelessness, which is dangerous. Choice B is incorrect because the employer does not have a duty to protect employees because of where they choose to park. In choice C, the employer tested the current air quality and found it to be acceptable, which constitutes fulfilling the duty to the employee to ensure workplace safety. A company is allowed to follow what is minimally required, so choice D can be eliminated.

43. The correct answer is A. The public interest theory of regulation says that government regulations are good when they consider the well-being of the general public. Business interest (choice B) is based on regulation that ensures fair competition. Choices C and D are government-based reasons for regulations—in other words, these theories support government regulation as a means of obtaining government revenue through such things as licensing fees, for example.

44. The correct answer is D. Business ethics includes much more than social responsibility. For example, financial fiduciary duty is also part of business ethics. Choice A is inaccurate because research has shown that socially responsible companies tend to do better, as both customers and shareholders are often drawn to a company because of its accountability in this area. The opposite of choice B is accurate. Social responsibility does include workers' well-being. It is for this reason that companies using slave labor are frowned upon. Choice C is inaccurate because social responsibility is not always morally superior to a business's need to make a profit. For example, a corporation that is heading towards bankruptcy has an obligation to its stakeholders to make a profit—in a moral, ethical manner.

45. The correct answer is B. Some warranties are invoked for such a short time period that they do not provide coverage up until the time of normal wear and tear. Thus, the consumer is not financially protected. However, the information obtained from customers on the warranty cards is sold to marketing firms. Choice A is incorrect because companies would fail if they had to provide unlimited warranties; there is no moral issue involved. Choice C is incorrect because the manner of doing business has changed greatly with e-commerce. However, some online companies are now beginning to pay for shipping and handling for product warranties. Choice D is incorrect because consumers do have recourse through the court system or public opinion when a company fails to fulfill a warranty claim.

46. **The correct answer is C.** According to Kohlberg's theory of moral development, an individual who sacrifices, even going against established law, to support a wider moral issue is in the post-conventional level of development. Choices A and B are earlier levels of moral development. Choice D is a stage within the pre-conventional level of moral development.

47. **The correct answer is A.** In a common trade agreement, even the country that is economically better off benefits from no tariffs on those country's imports and creates more opportunity within its owns borders. This opportunity develops from the need for added jobs in the areas of transportation and retailing. Choice B is incorrect because it is the economically better-off country that is being socially responsible by reducing costs for its neighboring countries. Choices C and D are arguments against trade agreements.

48. **The correct answer is B.** Whenever any individual treats a job candidate or an employee negatively because of bias, discrimination occurs. Choices A and D reflect biases that, unlike discrimination, work in the job candidate's favor. Equal opportunity (choice C) is an effort to eliminate bias or correct historical bias.

49. **The correct answer is D.** Utilitarianism is based upon the idea that moral actions come from decisions that bring the greatest happiness to the greatest number of people. Thinking globally does just that. Relativism and the social contract (choices A and C, respectively) are based upon moral decisions steeped in cultural norms of a society. There are so many different societies that there are no global values. Egoism (choice B) is based on self-interest.

50. **The correct answer is A.** A socially responsible corporation will pay what is known as a living wage, which is a wage that will allow the employee to live a decent life. However, even socially responsible corporations are not always able to pay that amount. Choice B is not true because any company is held legally liable to pay minimum wage, whether the company is socially responsible or not. Choice C is not entirely true as an employee does not owe loyalty to an employer if that employer is unethical. Choice D is inaccurate. Employees do owe loyalty, when appropriate, in addition to honesty and integrity.

51. The correct answer is D. Social responsibility refers to a company's acceptance of the role that ethics play in its business. Social responsibility also includes the company's obligations to consumer and societal well-being in relation to the company's performance and profits. Corporate philanthropy is one form of social responsibility.

52. The correct answer is B. Under the Foreign Corrupt Practices Act of 1977, lobbying that does not involve gifts or cash is allowed. The actions described in choices A, C, and D are in direct violation of the law.

53. The correct answer is C. Even if the recording is purely for the sake of quality assurance, the employer must still inform both the employee and the customer that the recording is taking place. Choice A is incorrect because the employer is not allowed to monitor phone conversations, even if there are issues with the employee, unless the employer notifies the employee of the monitoring that is taking place. Choice B does not include notification. Choice D is incorrect because in such cases where fraud is known, the employer should turn the information over to authorities.

54. The correct answer is D. Quality of life benefits include paid leave of absence, gym memberships, and other types of perks that allow an employee to have a good work/life balance. An employer is legally obligated to provide health insurance (choice A) to its employees. Most companies take out life insurance (choice B) on employees in order for the company to benefit. Not all companies can operate under flexible work schedules (choice C), and this type of benefit is one of many under the classification of quality-of-life benefits.

55. The correct answer is B. A union is a group of workers, not necessarily from the same company but usually in the same field of work, coming together for basic employment reasons. A mediator (choice A) is a disinterested third party that comes in to help settle a disagreement between a union and a company. An arbitrator (choice C) is similar to a mediator, except an arbitrator's decision is binding on both the union and the company. A striker (choice D) is someone who belongs to a union.

56. **The correct answer is D.** In Kohlberg's law and order level of moral development (the highest level in the conventional stage), an individual acts morally because they want to be accepted by those in authority. According to Maslow's theory, when the lower needs of life basics, safety, and belonging are met, an individual has a self-esteem need that needs to be fulfilled. This need is centered on being valued and recognized by others, such as those in authority. Psychological (choice A), safety (choice B), and social (choice C) needs are not tied to moral development.

57. **The correct answer is C.** In legal terms, sexual harassment involves both unwelcome and inappropriate actions of a sexual nature in the workplace. Choice A is not the best answer because it only mentions overt sexual advances; sexual harassment also includes inappropriate actions, such as leaving materials of sexual nature displayed in the workplace. Choice B is incorrect because sexual harassment is a type of sex discrimination, but sex discrimination also involves not hiring based on gender bias. Choice D is incorrect because the legality of sexual harassment involves the workplace only.

58. **The correct answer is A.** Egoism is based on actions that are in one's self-interest. If the employee is not concerned about the company's reaction, then their decision is based on what is in their best interest. Under utilitarianism (choice B), an employee would automatically use the points to get free work-related stays rather than personal stays, as there would be greater good in helping the company save money, which in turn improves profits and conditions for all stakeholders. Relativism is based on cultural norms, but we do not have any indication of what the cultural norm is from the information given, so choice C is not the best answer. The theory of deontology (choice D) would say the employee has a duty or obligation to the company.

59. **The correct answer is A.** While a corporation does have a fiduciary duty to the owners of the corporation to earn a profit, this duty does not include doing *anything* to grow profits, especially unethical actions. A corporation has a fiduciary duty to stockholders to grow profits in an ethical manner.

60. **The correct answer is C.** The Uniformed Services Employment Rights Act of 1993 was created because some companies started to refuse employment for those who were in the military reserves and who therefore would not be able to work while deployed. While the act does protect veteran's rights, choice A is incorrect because it also protects the rights of those obligated to serve. Choice B is incorrect because the law was created to prevent discrimination, not to ensure patriotism. Choice D is incorrect because the Vietnam Era Veterans Readjustment Act of 1974 was created to help disabled veterans.

Like what you see? Get unlimited access to Peterson's full catalog of DSST practice tests, instructional videos, flashcards, and more at **www.petersons.com/testprep/dsst**.

9 780768 944402